The Rail Holiday Maker

Scouring the planet for your next holiday

Rob Carroll

For Maeve, Erin and Clare

Chapters

Chapter 1 - From Matterhorn to Montreux – Glacier Express & Golden Pass

I can picture the scene vividly, even now. It was the first ever text message from my dad. He had just bought his first mobile phone. This was in 2005 and, to be fair, I too had only very reluctantly agreed to leave the analogue world behind around two years earlier, my wife heavily pregnant with our first child and the heavy load of real-life adult responsibility beginning to drop onto my shoulders.

My parents were not well-travelled. I always assumed that my own itchy feet and thirst for travel were born out of a childhood that, although contented and carefree, rarely ventured further than the nearby Yorkshire or Lincolnshire coastal resorts, dotted with static caravans, amusement arcades and kiss-me-quick hats. Those were idyllic family holidays in an era when we had to cut our cloth accordingly and I wouldn't change a thing; hunting for fossils on Filey Brig, wasting my bag of coppers in the bandits on the seafront, the patter of rain on the tin roof that was our shelter for the week. With their kids having fled the nest, my parents began to spread their own wings, purchasing a touring caravan and beginning a quest to explore this island, especially Scotland. Mum in particular developed a huge interest for all things Caledonian. So back to that first ever text message from dad:

'We are sitting in Fort William gazing at Ben Nevis.'

At this point I'm pretty ashamed to say that I had never been to Scotland. I had lived and worked abroad, and, working in the travel industry, had been fortunate to travel with work quite a bit already. But not to Scotland. Within a few years I would have more than rectified this with regular visits, a passion for all things Caledonian to match my mum's and an absolute basic need to be north of the border every once in a while. But that's another chapter. I wasn't in that place back then. And so my response to dad?

'I'm sitting in Zermatt gazing at the Matterhorn.'

Oh, how smug must I have felt tapping those words into my little Nokia?! I hadn't told dad I was going on a trip. And my mountain was definitely bigger than his. Ben Nevis indeed. I was on the balcony of my room in a cosy family-run chalet hotel in the car-free resort of Zermatt. This was an educational trip organised by the Swiss Tourist Board to promote the idea of travelling around Switzerland by rail. I was working at the time for a company that had been created from the merger of the UK's two biggest coach tour operators, both of which had offered the delights of the Glacier Express and the Bernina excursions for some time. But this was my own first experience of Swiss rail.

Why am I beginning my memoirs in Switzerland? Well, something happened that week that changed my life. If you have been on an organised rail holiday at some stage since 2005 it is quite possible that I designed it, tested it and made it possible. This rail tour of Switzerland sparked something and sent me off on my own journey. I'd like to take you along for a ride behind the scenes in the travel industry, with the triumphs and troubles, the highs and lows of making holidays happen. Along the way I'll describe the journeys too; great railway journeys will punctuate the story as they have punctuated a large chunk of my adult life.

It began in Zurich. I was joined by a few other tour operators, all of us identified as people who might give more brochure space to the Swiss. Having reclaimed our luggage from the carousel, Ivan from Switzerland Tourism handed me my Swiss Pass. 'What's a Swiss Pass?' you might be asking at this point. Well, imagine a golden ticket way beyond Willy Wonka's wildest dreams. If Switzerland were a chocolate factory (actually, many would say it is!), it would open the door to almost every delicious delight. But this book is about travel, not chocolate, and the Swiss Pass is the golden ticket that opens the door of trains, boats and buses on Switzerland's enviable integrated transport system. Our bags wouldn't be with us for long though as they would be checked in at the station, sent ahead and would be waiting for us at Zermatt station. How clever are the Swiss?!

Zermatt in the summer is a peaceful haven for walkers and mountaineers, with the combustion engine banned and only battery or electric powered vehicles permitted. I would have liked to lead you in gently to my story, but Ivan had other ideas. This was a packed itinerary and, no sooner had we arrived along the southern route of the Glacier Express, we were whisked onto the Gornergratbahn. If you like facts as much as I do, the Gornergratbahn is the highest open-air rack railway in Europe and, dating from 1898, the oldest electrical rack railway in Switzerland (and second oldest in the world). As the sun began to fall, we had amazing views of the Matterhorn all the way to the mountain station at the Gornergrat's summit, no less than 3,089 metres above sea level. That's more than twice the size of your mountain, dad! And the little Gornergrat is dwarfed by the mighty Matterhorn! Ben bloody Nevis!

I believe I just mentioned the Glacier Express in passing. 'What's going on here then?' you might be asking. The route between Brig and Zermatt forms part of one of the world's most famous excursions. How could I skip over it in such blasé fashion? Isn't this supposed to be a book about finding great railways to great destinations? Well, in my defence we would retrace our tracks to Brig on the Glacier Express the following day, before continuing along the second stretch of the Matterhorn Gotthardbahn to Andermatt as well. Though there are many descriptions of this famous journey, for the uninitiated I'm happy to oblige. It was, after all, my first time.

It is known as 'the world's slowest express train' and the route from Zermatt begins with a descent down the Mattertal Valley to Visp, with mighty rocks either side of the narrow valley and racks used to help the train grip the tracks on the steepest sections. From Brig to Andermatt, where we would leave the train, the scenery opens up into everyone's idea of the perfect Swiss idyll, following the Rhône Valley through a natural landscape of mountains, meadows, flower-adorned houses and hamlets. As we were guests of the Matterhorn Gotthardbahn railway company, we were treated to lunch on board as sensational scenery outside our panoramic windows gradually became the norm. There was schnapps involved too. Could this trip possibly get any better?

In Switzerland transportation is complicated yet simultaneously effortless. Changing trains at Andermatt, we headed down to Göschenen. Changing again here, the next part of the descent uses another masterpiece of Swiss engineering, a series of spiral tunnels around the village of Wassen, cutting deep through the mountains, peeping occasionally back into daylight to get your bearings before the next tunnel deep into the Alps. We eventually reached the lakeside at Flüelen, where, of course, the boat was waiting for the train's arrival. Everything really does run like clockwork. What a perfect way to end an exhilarating day, relaxing on board a Lake Lucerne ship, gently navigating our way across the lake known locally as Vierwaldstättersee (lake of the four wooded cantons!) to Lucerne itself.

I've been back to Lucerne several times since this trip. It is arguably Switzerland's most attractive large town, with its wooden covered bridges and quaint alleys opening out to the lakeside quays from which some of the great Swiss excursions begin, such as the Rigi round trip or the Pilatus round trip, combining boats with once-a-lifetime mountain railway experiences. Lining the lakeside are some pretty swish hotels, one of which, the Art Deco Hotel Montana, boasts the world's shortest funicular railway (did I mention that I like facts?), linking the lakeside with the hotel lobby. I know this because I went back a few years later and arranged a contracting visit to the hotel, with no intention of actually contracting it, purely to ride on its funicular. You have probably gathered that after this tour I started to like trains. A lot.

This was a trip of superlatives and our designated hotel in Lucerne's city centre provided me with another first. On opening my case my shirts were now too crumpled to retain any self-respect that evening. I was sure the imperfection of creases would be frowned upon in perfect Switzerland and so I popped to Reception to request an iron. This being logical, efficient Switzerland I wasn't allowed to take such fire-starting equipment to my room, so they logically and efficiently set up a board for me right next to Reception. I doubt this experience will be repeated, standing next to Reception in a 4* hotel with an ironing board, ironing my shirts. I swear that, given a bit more time, I might have made a few Francs from people checking in and admiring the hotel's very visible ironing service.

There was no time for side hustles on this tour though. There was barely time to catch your breath before it was taken away again by the next awe-inspiring experience. A new day, a new dream journey. The Golden Pass Line connects Lucerne with Montreux via Interlaken, requiring changes, but offering an incredible variety of scenery through high alpine Bernese Oberland to swish and chic Lake Geneva. The first section from Lucerne to Interlaken begins with lakes and hills before climbing over the beautiful Brünig Pass, then descending to the northern shore of Lake Brienz, hugging the lakeside all the way to Interlaken Ost, one of Switzerland's great interchange stations.

As its name suggests, Interlaken sits between two lakes, Brienz and Thun. Leaving the town, the line skirts the southern shore of Lake Thun, with fabulous views from the right-hand side of the train as it heads for Spiez and Zweisimmen. From here the train climbs up to the steepest part of the line at Saanenmöser (1,279 metres – are you paying attention, dad?!) before hitting the high-end mountain resort of Gstaad, playground of the rich and famous.

I haven't mentioned the train! Oh my goodness, the train! We were fortunate to have first class Swiss Passes and reserved seats on the Golden Pass Panoramic train, with those panoramic windows enhancing one of the most beautiful rail journeys in the world. What's more, on this train the driver sits elevated above you in a little cab, leaving the front seats for travellers. I had the driver's eye view and panoramic windows! This journey changed my life.

As the Golden Pass train twisted and descended through the lush vineyards towards distant and tempting Lake Geneva, I had a eureka moment. A travelling companion showed me his employer's brochure, with an impressive selection of escorted rail holidays. It hadn't occurred to me that rail holidays could be a thing. A voice inside me screamed, 'That's what I'm going to do!' And within a year I was doing just that, working for the world's largest rail holiday company, travelling all over the place by train, dreaming up next year's new tours. And the very first one was my homage to the Golden Pass Line, which, for me at least, still beats the other long-distance and more celebrated Swiss rail journeys.

At Montreux we descended the escalator and crossed the road into the convenient and splendid Grand Hotel Suisse Majestic, an ornate and opulent grand lakeside hotel from the Belle Époque era that would also be the first hotel I would sign up for my next employer. Gazing across the lake I wasn't to know what was in store. Within a couple of months the grand old lady of Yorkshire coach travel, Wallace Arnold, was closed down and my colleagues and I had to find new paths to tread. My next path would actually be a train track thanks to Ivan, Swiss Tourism and Switzerland's amazing, inspiring railways. Merci vielmal!

Chapter 2 - The Arctic Circle Train

The Arctic Circle Train? Blimey, if those words in combination don't conjure up a certain level of anticipation, then possibly you are reading the wrong book! For the next chapter we will have to fast forward around eighteen months from the Swiss trip. But first, here's a short interlude.

Redundancy had been a shock to the system, with Mrs C on a break from her own travel career, a toddler and a newborn baby at home. An interim job came along as Hotel Contractor at a big hotel booking company in York. I didn't stay long. Living in Leeds I could compare it with Brian Clough's time as Leeds United manager, although I did manage more than Cloughie's 44 days. But it wasn't the right fit for me, running from hotel to hotel agreeing rates for stag and hen parties.

My third and last trip for them was to the exquisitely beautiful Baltic capitals, Tallinn and Riga, at that time recently discovered by budget airlines bringing gangs of revellers from all over Britain for weekends of cheap booze and other cheap thrills. Riga is an Art Nouveau gem and Tallinn was a delight at an icy cold -17 degrees, dressed to chill in its February winter coat. I remember trudging uphill through the thick snow after work to its Old Town, a mesmerising mix of Scandinavia, central Europe and Russia in one bundle of buildings, collection of courtyards. But my overriding memory is of the last hotel, out by the airport and just before my flight home. Weary from running between ten or twelve hotels a day, I was invited into a dingy back-office to wait for the General Manager. After a few minutes she arrived, a fearsome looking older woman, well-built, stern-faced and ready to do battle over room rates. She sat down and gave me a piercing stare.

'So...you...are....from.........Piss-Up?' growled the voice on the opposite side of the desk, almost spitting out each syllable with disdain, particularly the last two.

'Did she just say what I think she said?!' I asked myself. With beer at around £1 a pint it had been quite a good trip, and I do like a beer or two after work sometimes, but how the hell did she know?! Had they got someone following me? Did the KGB still operate in these parts?

There was (in fact there still is) a company called pissup.com organising breaks for stag parties in Tallinn, boozy weekends with strip shows and Kalashnikov shooting. Really not my kind of thing. Somehow, I held it together. I managed to lift my jaw from the ground and look back at her stony face. I managed not to roll on the floor in a fit of juvenile giggles. The lady just said 'Piss-Up'!! Instead, I protested my innocence. No, I wasn't from Piss-Up; I was a respectable family man.

Soon afterwards my dream job came along at the world's largest rail tour operator. After a few initial trips out to check hotels in various places, the Arctic Circle Train would be the first big trip. And so, setting the scene, I was now in Stockholm and feeling pretty damned pleased with myself actually. Maybe I pinched myself to check that it was really happening. A train beyond the Arctic Circle. My very own Polar Express.

This was to be a quick (barely) four-day trip, more about quality control than anything else. The overnight sleeper train from Stockholm to Narvik had not been well received by customers, even though for most, me included, the mere thought of it would conjure up a journey of adventure and excitement to a wild, scarcely populated part of Europe. The train would depart Stockholm just before 6pm, chugging along the eastern coast of Sweden as we slept, before waking up with the momentous box-ticking exercise of crossing the Arctic Circle. It would then continue along western Europe's northernmost railway line across the Norwegian border, reaching the strategic seaport of Narvik some 1,120 km later. A remarkable journey, an adventure most certainly, but perhaps a bit of an endurance test too?

I had flown into Stockholm Arlanda, taken the Arlanda Express train from the airport to Stockholm Central, done my duty of checking out the hotels in the station's vicinity, all ready for the main event. This was a journey I had longed to experience, even though the customer questionnaires had told a different story. That it was late February and already dark added to the mystique. To hammer home just how committed I was, I would spend that night on the sleeper train to Narvik, then one night in Narvik itself, before returning on the sleeper to Stockholm the following night. That's 2,240 km of sleeper train in three days, folks! Committed? Maybe it was time for me to be committed!

Why did I feel so smug then? It was dark outside and there wouldn't be much to see as the train headed north. Well, that was true but my colleagues had booked me a compartment and I'd found my lower bunk. If you have never been on a sleeper train in Europe, this was similar to many, a plastic pod with lower bunk and an upper bunk that would pull out from the wall. There was a window with pull down blind, with a small table protruding beneath the window which, with the lid lifted, doubled as a sink. Toilets and showers were down the corridor, as with most wagons lits. I had with me the autobiography of the late great radio DJ John Peel, a book he had begun to write before his untimely death whilst on holiday at altitude in the Andes and completed with love by his family. It had been a Christmas present from Mrs C, but with two toddlers now at home reading for pleasure had become a thing of the past. Here was my chance to make inroads, a simple pleasure as the train headed into the wintry night. I'd raided the shop at the station and invested in a big bowl of ham salad and a couple of cans of local beer. Yes indeed, simple pleasures and splendid isolation. A few hours of peace, quiet and a little bit of 'me time' before waking up in a land of wilderness beyond the Arctic Circle.

As we pulled out of Stockholm Central my idyll was broken. There was a knock on the compartment door. It wasn't the guard. The chap politely introduced himself as Ahmed. He didn't speak English, I don't speak Persian, but we managed a pleasant conversation in German in which he dropped the bombshell that he had booked the top bunk. I hadn't reckoned with this scenario. Now maybe I'm being a bit of a diva here, but I had mistakenly thought my colleagues had booked me a whole compartment, not a bloody bed in a shared cabin! The older you get (and I was mid-30s at that time), the less appealing it becomes to share your living space, let alone sleeping space, with a complete stranger. Neither did it seem particularly appealing or fair to scoff my ham salad and swig my way through a couple of cans of lager in front of my unexpected travelling companion, who had already made himself comfortable in the pull-out contraption beneath the ceiling. I retired instead to the seating carriages, eventually creeping into bed for a restless night, with the train's soothing rhythms jolted by my room-mate's snores. Using the term 'sleeper' for this kind of train is, for me at least, a misnomer.

Who needs sleep anyway?! At around 7am we reached Boden, a rail junction about 50 miles away from the Arctic Circle, where the train halted for a while. There was snow on the ground as I stretched my legs in the icy early morn, not straying too far from the train, lest it depart without me, leaving me waiting hours for the next one in the freezing cold. We duly crossed the Arctic Circle (tick!) and approached Kiruna in Swedish Lapland, where I had decided to break my journey for around four hours. Our customers did this very thing as part of their tour, albeit during the summer months. Kiruna is a working town with iron ore mines dominating the local economy. Our customers were generally whisked away from industrial Kiruna to visit the village of Jukkasjärvi to meet reindeer and have lunch in a Sami community. In winter though Kiruna is a completely different beast, with the slag heaps, a scene so familiar from my youth in the South Yorkshire coalfields, covered in a thick layer of glistening white snow and nearby Jukkasjärvi boasting a temporary building that would excite quite a few of you, at least I hope it would.

I'm talking about the Ice Hotel! Yes, a hotel sculpted from blocks of ice, not the kind of thing you get to see every day. Now, as part of my job I've had the pleasure of being shown round hundreds of hotels by keen and exuberant Sales Managers, often viewing identikit rooms with essentially the same features and facilities. This was to be a hotel show-round with a difference. The rooms were all different, all works of art, glistening and beautifully carved into the ice. The Ice Bar was something else too, though having been led to the icy counter sadly there was no time to sample the wares as my guide, Gunnar, was keen to get me back to Kiruna. I was told that a different construction was created every year for the winter season as the hotel melts when the summer arrives. Adjacent to the cold comfort of the Ice Hotel is a permanent structure with extra rooms for those not wishing to sleep in an animal skin on a bed of ice, plus a renowned restaurant to warm your hearts and fill your stomachs with local produce. In a region so harsh in climate they really do make the best of what manages to grow.

Back in Kiruna, the church (kyrka) is one of Sweden's largest wooden buildings and well worth a visit. Having checked out the small number of hotels that might be suitable for future customers, I rejoined the next train to Narvik. This line, the Ofotbanen, is the northernmost in western Europe and was opened way back in 1903 specifically to enable the rich pickings of iron ore from Kiruna to reach an ice-free seaport across the Norwegian border at Narvik. It's hard to believe that, prior to the railway, reindeer were used to make this epic journey. It's also impossible to imagine the hardships suffered by those brave souls who built this railway through some of Europe's most hostile terrain and in severe winters. In the strange twilight of a Swedish Lapland emerging from winter's darkest depths, the train skirted the vast shoreline of the Torneträsk lake, dropping off skiers and adventurers at Abisko and Björkliden, now very much synonymous with Northern Lights seekers through the winter months. What followed was an amazing snowbound climb up to the mountain resort of Riksgrensen, the last stop before the Norwegian border (its name translates as 'border of the realm'), before twisting and turning on a descent to the alluring Rombaksfjord and finally the Ofotfjord and our journey's end, Narvik.

I would highly recommend the night train beyond the Arctic Circle (now operated by Vy) for anyone looking for an adventure but without luxury. It is certainly a great journey. However, for anyone with a little more time to spend, there are other ways of reaching Narvik from Stockholm by train, splitting the journey, discovering more and seeing everything in daylight.

Narvik, whilst not the centre of the universe, has enough interest to spend a day or two, especially if you are a winter sports enthusiast. Aside from its main raison d'être as an industrial port, exporting the iron ore mined in Kiruna and sent across the mountains on the very route I had just ridden, the Narvikfjellet's slopes are accessed in minutes using the lifts close to Narvik's town centre. For those seeking less active experiences, the Museum Nord is based in the former NSB (Norwegian Railway) offices and traces the history of the Ofoten Railway, the remarkable navvies who built it against the odds and the development of Narvik as an ice-free harbour. Narvik's other major museum, the War Museum, homes in on the biggest land and sea battle of World War II, which took place between April and June 1940 between the Nazi and Allied forces, events that have scarred local memories to this day.

After my night in one of Narvik's small supply of comfortable hotels I rejoined the sleeper train to Stockholm the following afternoon, I have to admit with a certain amount of trepidation. Departing again in that strange twilight at around 3.15pm, I found my sleeper compartment, settled onto my bottom bunk and waited for the inevitable arrival of my as yet unknown room-buddy for the night. Right on time the train trundled away from Narvik, with no takers for the top bunk. 'Get in! I've got the whole cabin this time!' I thought to myself. Out came the John Peel autobiography, a pre-packed sandwich and a tin of Norwegian beer. The small joys of a life on the road (erm, I mean rails).

As we slowly made our way through the snow towards Sweden I wandered carefree along the train to find the best spot from which to take in the increasingly snowbound scenery and empty, remote stations before total darkness fell, at which point I would retire to my cabin for a restful evening. How very civilised. I could really get used to this. My plans were shattered at Riksgrensen, the first station in Sweden, where a platoon of Swedish national servicemen boarded the train. Returning to my compartment, I was hit by a double whammy. I hadn't previously noticed that there were in fact two pull-out berths above my bottom bunk. And they were both now occupied. On the bunk directly above me, just inches from my nose, wriggled a lad in khaki with the worst cold in Scandinavia. On the top bunk another khaki clad youth gave me a surly stare, then continued to strum 'Wonderwall' by Oasis on his acoustic guitar, complete with comedy Swedish Mancunian accent. The sleeper train chugged and juddered, my near neighbour coughed and spluttered, the surly youth strummed and muttered. It was the longest night of my travelling life.

Chapter 3 - Caledonia Dreaming Part 1

This chapter is about Scotland. It won't be the last, believe me. But where do I begin? I started this chapter several times, then scrapped each and every one. My favourite destination of all is also the hardest one to write about.

I grew up in the north of England. That's not very far from Scotland. Considering the miles of track I've ridden and the miles of road I've driven searching for your next holiday, can someone please explain to me why I reached the age of 36 before finally venturing north of the border for the first time?

I love music. In fact, I've even put many music tours together. Classical Music tours to central Europe. Blues, Jazz & Rock 'n' Roll tours to the Deep South USA. Beatles tours as well. But Glasgow is my favourite music city bar none. "What about Liverpool?" shrieks my parents' generation. "What about Manchester?" shrieks my own generation. People of various generations in the States may, with reason, insert Memphis or Nashville or New Orleans or Chicago or Detroit or San Francisco. But for this ageing indie-kid the Glasgow sound prevails. I won't bore you with the detail. But if I were to name my top 20 bands ten of them would be from Glasgow and its surrounding new towns. It's a city crackling with atmosphere and sublime architecture that hopefully recent tragic fires won't destroy. But I didn't make it there until my late 30s. So what took me so long?

My parents spread their wings ever so slightly when my sister and I fled their Rotherham nest. A second-hand touring caravan was purchased and off they went to join the legion of slow moving and slightly precarious looking vehicles blocking the road to those of us hopelessly stuck behind and already late for our next meeting with a disgruntled hotelier. Fairly soon they made it to Scotland and the scene was set for many wonderful holidays, just dad, mum and the dog. Mum would stock up the van with military precision and off they would go. The route was well worn. The A1 through North Yorkshire, then get your snail-paced caravan-towing kicks on Route 66 (that's the A66 with a little poetic license!), the M6 past the Lake District and across the border for the first night's stopover in the village that sounds like a half-heard expletive at Scottish pub closing time, Ecclefechan. The following day would see them clogging up the narrow road skirting the bonnie banks of Loch Lomond, then continuing their never-ending crawl through majestic Glencoe (the greatest road journey on this island?) or through the lochs and glens to the coast at Oban, a town that became my mum's favourite on this planet. When mum gained an interest in something she would pursue it with vigour and over the years she became a fount of all knowledge for all things Scottish, so deep was her love.

Me? Well, I was busy discovering exciting new places in the name of work. They could keep their Scotland, my old folks, because I was ticking off places way more interesting. Or so I thought. That was due to change and with an almighty bang. I was working for a rail tour company that specialised in holidays all over Europe and the world, yet had never attempted a tour in the UK. Finally, we had devised our first domestic itinerary, a circular tour of Scotland that still exists all these years later, and I had two trips booked to recce the routes and hotels. A break from the norm and exciting times ahead.

Then the phone rang in the middle of the night. A phone call at that time is never going to bear good news. My parents had set off with their touring caravan on the first day of their latest jaunt around Scotland. They had broken their journey, as usual, in Ecclefechan. I may have mentioned already that its name sounds like a collection of profanities and I've passed it many times since, usually profaning loudly myself, cursing the place where my mum died suddenly that night in early June 2007. Prior to my planned first visits to Scotland, my real first trip across the border was to bring my dad home. I swear it felt like the longest journey of my life, trying to hold it together for him.

Two weeks later, still overcome with grief, I was in Inverness. The following months and years of covering every piece of tarmac, and every iron road too, brought me a connection with my mum that I'll always treasure, as I discovered bit by bit exactly why she was so smitten with Scotland, then set out to fill holiday brochures with my new darling with almost evangelical fervour.

To get to Inverness I had experienced for the first time the delights of the East Coast Mainline northbound from York. If you have never done it, it is arguably the best mainline journey in the country from York northwards. The friendly Northeast greets you with a great aerial view of historic Durham, before the Tyne Bridges come into view as you enter handsome Newcastle. What follows are long stretches of unspoilt sandy beaches, the criminally uncredited coastline of Northumberland with the mysterious and spiritual Farne Islands in the distance offshore. I've only ever passed through Berwick-upon-Tweed, but every time I look down at the town from the track I remind myself that I must stop there some time. A quick jaunt inland and you arrive at Edinburgh Waverley, the station sprawled across the bed splitting the tourist heartthrob of the Royal Mile from the bustling retail queen of Princes Street.

As we wait to change trains at Waverley this seems like a timely interlude to discuss the merits of the so-called 'Central Belt'. I've already expressed why I love Glasgow, but Edinburgh is probably the greatest city on this island. It has it all. A place rammed with tourists is usually rammed with tourists for a reason, yet in all my visits there since I've never felt the crowds to be intrusive. It's walkable (if hilly), young, jam-packed with life and culture. And it has a great record shop for vinyl lovers like me, 'Unknown Pleasures' down High Street, just about doable if you have an hour between trains.

On this trip I wasn't alone and probably with good reason considering recent events. My young German colleague Claudia (still a great friend, so I must be a decent travelling companion) had accompanied me to get some experience and help me fit as much as possible into a short space of time. Plus, we'd managed to charm the Orient Express into letting us use two unsold rooms on their Royal Scotsman train for a couple of nights! But let's not get ahead of ourselves. If you haven't travelled the line northwards from Edinburgh to Inverness, it's another gem of a rail journey.

You have two choices of route. The first is to continue with the East Coast Mainline operator (whoever owns the franchise this week) on a long-distance inter-city train via Stirling, but I would recommend a second option. Scotrail runs a regular, more commuter-style service between the two cities, but their route takes you over the Firth of Forth across the UNESCO World Heritage masterpiece Forth Bridge. The Highland Line from Perth roughly follows the A9, but why keep your eyes on the road ahead when you can gaze at the Grampians from a train? The names now trip off my tongue like old friends. Dunkeld & Birnam, Pitlochry, Blair Atholl, Newtonmore, Dalwhinnie, Kingussie, Aviemore, Carrbridge and Inverness.

After the following day visiting Inverness hotels, we took a train back to Aviemore for dinner, where my German companion chose a Yorkshire Pudding filled with haggis. A taxi transported us to Boat of Garten on the Strathspey Steam Railway line to join the Royal Scotsman, half-way through its 4 day rail cruise, mooring for the night with after dinner drinks in the ornate bar. There seemed to be more staff on board the train than guests and, although their service was undoubtedly attentive and incredibly professional, this boy from Rotherham was slightly unnerved by all the forelock-tugging.

When we met our fellow guests we understood. The high ticket price of this 4 day trip (around £4,000 per person back then, if my memory serves me correctly) attracted a customer from a different planet to Rotherham. And I don't mean Barnsley. There was the nouveau riche Russian family who kept themselves to themselves because of the language barrier. A diminutive but stout middle-aged Texan millionaire with side-parting, seemingly transported directly from a 1980s Dallas film set, was talking about himself loudly by the bar. Sadly, his wife didn't get to speak. Three middle-aged female New Yorkers, who had been dropped off in Edinburgh for a few days by their golfer husbands, were also talking loudly about themselves and about being 'cougars'. Amidst the spectacle of self-aggrandisement on rails stood poor Claudia and I, plus a lovely couple from Lancashire, wide-eyed with their taster of how the other half live, whose children had bought this special experience as a gift for their 25th wedding anniversary. Come to think of it, thank heavens for that lovely couple from Lancashire!

My bedroom was superb, as was the train itself, the crew's service and the food too, rustled up in a tiny train galley. At breakfast we were quizzed by the 'cougars'. Just who is this mysterious duo who stepped aboard last night? Unfussed by the speculation, my teutonic travelling companion tucked into her breakfast haggis (haggis number two, Claudia!) and later we set off southwards through the Cairngorms towards Perth. You know the score - Aviemore, Kingussie, Dalwhinnie - and the malt was flowing in the bar car. The Texan millionaire was talking loudly about himself at the bar, the 'cougars' were talking loudly about their forthcoming hotel stay in Edinburgh ("at the Bal-mo-rahhhhhl") and the lovely Lancashire couple were ensconced in their well-earned luxury trip of a lifetime. And inside of me a silent but volatile rage simmered perilously close to the surface, threatening to scream, "STOP TALKING ABOUT YOURSELVES AND LOOK OUT OF THE BLOODY WINDOW. YOU ARE MISSING SOME OF THE BEST BLOODY SCENERY ON THIS ISLAND!"

But I didn't say it. Of course I didn't. I'm way too polite. Instead, we moored for the night in a siding at Perth station, had dinner (haggis number 3 within 24 hours, Claudia!) listening to the droning sounds of the self-obsessed, after which I escaped the confines of the train and pounded the proud streets of Perth in the mid-evening drizzle to let off steam.

Two weeks later I was back again, back to reconnect with my mum, this time in the western Highlands and it was there that I really fell in love with Scotland, just as she had done. Glencoe, the West Highland Line, Oban and the islands, white sands, lochs and glens, and deep forested ravines where you could close your eyes, open them again and swear you were in the Canadian Rockies. The sound of nothing but nature in the raw. But that's another chapter. As they say up there, 'Haste ye back.'

Chapter 4 - Caledonia Dreaming Part 2

P eople often ask me to name my favourite destination. Of all the places I could choose Scotland is closest to my heart for very personal reasons. I did make haste. Very soon I was back again north of the border. Two weeks later, in fact, and just weeks after my mum had left us. Mum had passed away a few miles beyond the Scottish border. It was as if she was determined to leave us in her favourite country. But only just. The following weeks included my first travels around Scotland, piecing together a grand tour of Scotland, but also dealing with my loss head-on. During the following years I covered every piece of tarmac, every iron road, soon sharing an intense love of Scotland with my mum and preaching all things Caledonian to the world through the medium of holiday brochures. This chapter is proof that something very lovely can develop from even the most desperately sad moments. It's my love letter to Scotland.

It had been a whirlwind few weeks since I had received that terrible phone call. I'd brought my dad back from Ecclefechan, the village that even sounds like a curse, the morning after that wretched night. Then a week or so later I was up in Inverness and Edinburgh researching the first half of the tour. But it was the next trip that blew me away and made me return again and again. And again.

I'll let you into a secret. I drove my car on this one. But I've ridden the tracks since and will describe those too, because the West Highland Line is a special draw. Armed with CDs I left Yorkshire at the crack of dawn, following my parents' well-trodden path up the A1, Route 66 (yes, the A66 really, I know, but I am Caledonia dreaming!), then the M6 northwards. My soundtrack would be Scottish Indie from Orange Juice through to the Pastels and Teenage Fanclub to the Delgados, but with the addition of a recent bargain bucket find from York's now long-gone Track Records, 'Sweetheart of the Rodeo' by the Byrds under the heavy Country influence of Gram Parsons. Cursing loudly at Ecclefechan as I passed, I circumnavigated Glasgow, but wasn't prepared for the jaw-dropping scenery ahead as the roads opened out towards mountains, lochs and glens.

Once you are past Dumbarton the scenery begins to unfold, skirting Loch Lomond en route to Crianlarich, a strange village with a hotel, a shop and a church that hosts a service a couple of times a month. Crianlarich is an eerie junction town for road and rail. It is here that the West Highland Line splits into its western branch to Oban and northern branch to Fort William and eventually Mallaig. The road follows a similar path westwards, but the northern route takes in different terrain to the railway. I hit a left for Oban, mum's favourite place on Earth.

So, I've just described a beautiful journey in terms of roads and towns. What about the scenery? Well, with your eyes on the road the scenery is a backdrop but not a focal point, an ever-changing mix of colour and wilderness. It is so different by train. ScotRail's services leave Glasgow Queen Street, following a similar route at first, then deviating to provide almost instant pleasure. The first part of the journey northwards on the West Highland Line is dominated by water. The Firth of Clyde provides the first sea views, followed by Gareloch and a journey along the eastern shore of Loch Long, a 20 mile long sea loch. From Arrochar and Tarbet, with glimpses of Loch Lomond's bonnie northern banks, you feel you are really heading into the Highlands, all deep forests as you climb to Crianlarich. The western branch to Oban then ticks every box for those seeking lochs and glens. Loch Awe is so aptly named and the track runs along the northern shore whilst those travelling by car see little of the loch from the heavily tree-lined road above. Nearby Cruachan mountain hides within it a secret masterpiece of engineering, a hydro-electric power station buried deep within the mountain. Next up is the 'little ugly one', or Loch Etive, another 20 mile long sea loch that is far from ugly. At the Falls of Lora the Connel Bridge rolls into view, the place where my parents would plonk their caravan, looking out across the shore, as we make our way into Oban, a rail terminus but a busy hub for onward ferries to the Hebrides.

Oban is a renowned difficult spot in which to find group accommodation. There were a couple of hotels owned by coach operators. I remember knocking on the locked door of one of them. When the groups were all out on excursions, the hotel would shut up shop. The person looking at me with suspicion from the other side of the glass, unwilling to unlock the door, seemed to consider me more of an intruder than a person trying to bring them business. Other than this there are probably four suitable hotels, all with their foibles. The one in which I stayed the night was in my mind just about okay for our customers until I left my room the following morning to witness the bizarreness of the housekeeping staff's equipment. The hotel had invested in used and battered Tesco shopping trolleys to carry the cleaning materials, new bedding, towels and toiletries. Not a good sign.

Having exhausted all opportunities in Oban, having chosen the better of the hotels for our groups, I drove along the coast to Fort William via Ballachulish along the shores of Loch Linnhe. Dropping my stuff at the Alexandra Hotel in Fort William, pretty much a one-street town under the watchful gaze of Ben Nevis, I visited the other hotels. At the reception of the final one at the other end of Fort William's High Street I greeted the receptionist.

'Yes Madam,' came the reply.

Stroking my supposedly manly beard, I explained the purpose of my visit, which didn't turn out to be a long one, if I'm honest, but at least it provided a small comedy moment and, well, I needed the odd chuckle.

In my youth I had a period with long hair, particularly during the year I spent in Germany as part of my German degree when I didn't visit a 'Friseur' once. On my day off I would travel to Bremerhaven to pick up the previous week's NME from the only newsagent in the region that stocked foreign titles. I'd then generally devour it in a local bar, but on one sunny day I sat on a wooden deckchair on Theodor

Heuss Square, minding my own business, when an elderly man approached me with the words:

'Sind Sie ein Herr oder sind Sie eine Dame?'

I'm sure I don't need to translate that for you. Anyway, back to Fort William, still chuckling at being mistaken for a bearded lady, I jumped back in the car and headed north. This was a road trip after all. In the evening sun I drove two hours across the wild western Highlands to Kyle of Lochalsh, overlooking Skye across the strait, returning as the sun was setting. The roads were empty, the colours of the heather iridescent in the setting sun, amidst rocky terrain and gushing clear mountain waters, punctuated by viewpoints where you just had to stop to admire scenery that has no peer on these islands.

My ulterior motive was to call in unannounced at the hotel where Michael Palin had stayed on his 'Great Railway Journey of the World' to Kyle of Lochalsh. On arrival the sparse staff were busying themselves with a large German group that was almost bursting out of their small dining room. There was seemingly nobody at the reception counter, so I rang the bell. Immediately a head popped up from nowhere with the thickest jam jar glasses I have ever seen. Oh crumbs, here we go again. I managed the manliest of voices I could muster, but my request to see a room was still brusquely refused. Whilst the hotel was no great shakes, that evening I became completely smitten with the wild allure of the western Highlands, if not their hoteliers. I would venture north again and again to grapple with them, enjoying journeys through scenery of quite devastating beauty.

The route home was no less awesome. From Fort William the road leads through mighty Glencoe. Passing the excellent Glencoe Visitor Centre, the glen cuts through towering mountains on both sides of the road and climbs some 1,000 feet. Edging Rannoch Moor, the road rejoins the rail route at Bridge of Orchy before the junction at Crianlarich.

The northern branch of the West Highland Line (connecting Glasgow to Fort William and Mallaig) is for me the greatest of all railway journeys on these islands. Whilst the line's infamy reaches across the world with Harry Potter, the Glenfinnan Viaduct and Jacobite Steam Train, and rightly so, these attractions on the West

Highland Line are on the remote section between Fort William and the coastal fishing port of Mallaig, gazing out to the Hebrides. It is a remarkable journey, beginning with Neptune's Staircase of locks on the Caledonian Canal at Banavie, slowing for the drama of crossing the Glenfinnan Viaduct, with majestic Loch Shiel dominating the glen below, the Glenfinnan Monument proudly commemorating the Jacobite Risings. As the single track heads towards the coast, the Small Isles, Rhum, Eigg and Muck, tantalise in the distance, leaping in and out of view. It is a terrain of stark beauty, but with the promise of white sands, the sounds of nature and the best fish and chips in sleepy Mallaig, with Skye a stone's throw away across the Sound of Sleat.

But it's not the best bit! For me the line between Glasgow and Fort William has it all. From Glasgow ScotRail's Fort William bound trains feature the same wonderful scenery as Oban trains - the Firth of Clyde, Gareloch, Loch Long and Loch Lomond - but whereas the Oban trains hit a left through the lochs and glens I described earlier, the northern branch climbs into real Highlands as bleak as they are beguiling. North of Crianlarich there is a feat of engineering, the Horseshow Curve beneath mighty Ben Dorain, the track circling the glen to master the terrain. Next up is Rannoch Moor, where the track floats on peat boglands across the high heather moorland, a scene of desolate beauty, so remote from our existence that no roads lead here. Deer scamper into the distance at the intrusion of human life in a scene of idyllic and splendid isolation. The track now following a vastly different and wilder route to the road, we tick off Corrour, the highest altitude station in the UK, backdrop of the remote scenes of the film 'Trainspotting' and built originally to serve the nearby Corrour estate in the early days of tourism, when visitors would leave the cities for a weekend of hunting on the Highland moors. At journey's end is Fort William, nestled beneath Ben Nevis, dad's mountain and the highest on this island.

Whenever I find myself on the ScotRail trains that service these routes I'm always impressed, but left dreaming. Dreaming that ScotRail (or someone!) might hook a panoramic carriage onto the train like they do in Switzerland, with windows stretching to the sky, haggis, neeps and tatties served to your table and a wee dram of single malt to finish as Ben Nevis lunges into view. Think 'Glacier Express'. Then imagine 'Glenfinnan Express'. How could it be anything other than a roaring success?! Maybe I am just Caledonia Dreaming, but I keep coming back. I love this place. Thank you mum.

Chapter 5 - A Night Train to Warsaw

B erlin Lichtenberg of an evening is a bit spooky. Or at least it was back then. This would have been around 2008, with the credit crunch in full swing and a trip to Poland designed to renegotiate hotel rates or to find less expensive versions. The company was looking to tighten its belt a little bit after years of success.

I've been back to Lichtenberg since. Actually, I've been back a few times as it has historic sites off the beaten Berlin track that are rarely visited but which I find immensely thought-provoking. On one edge of this starkly eastern suburb, a short walk from the wonderfully named 'Avenue of the Cosmonauts', sits the 'Memorial to the Socialists', the resting place of the good and the not-so-good comrades in East Germany's socialist and soviet past. It really is well worth a couple of hours of exploration, as long as you know what you are looking for and if, like me, you like to hang around in graveyards every once in a while.

The site is massive, with sections poignantly remembering volunteers who went to fight Franco in Spain, as well as those who stood against the Nazis, paying the highest price for their beliefs. The last time I visited (I've hung around this graveyard more than once!) I stumbled upon just one typical story at the not particularly prominent grave of Willi Schneider, born in 1907 and killed on 1st January 1931, not yet 24 years of age. A sales assistant, Willi was part of the Social Democratic Party as well as a cross-party organisation protecting the democracy of Germany's Weimar Republic from right-wing and left-wing extremists. During the night of New Year's Eve Willi was shot by Hitler's 'Sturmabteilung' henchmen. At his funeral, which became a mass demonstration in favour of parliamentary democracy, the Social Democrat MP Johannes Stelling called for an end to, 'the murder of people who fight for their beliefs using only spiritual weapons'. Stelling himself was murdered by the SA in 1933 and rests within this very same graveyard.

There is also a 'Revolution Monument' commemorating the failed Spartacist uprising of 1919. The centrepiece of the site, the 'Memorial to the Socialists' itself, houses the graves of those Spartacist leaders, Rosa Luxemburg and Karl Liebknecht, Communist revolutionaries during the civil war that gripped Berlin, killed by a militia called the Freikorps, ironically ordered to quash the rebellion by the Social Democrats. That's not the biggest irony though, as the Soviet regime that followed World War II also buried its Politburo members in this cemetery, which means that revolutionary Rosa Luxemburg, idolised and idealised by many, rests not too far away from Walter Ulbricht, the GDR leader responsible for the Berlin Wall that cruelly split families and friends for decades. Fittingly, a small stone on a nearby large, grassed area remembers the victims of Stalinism.

The 'Memorial to the Socialists' is part of Lichtenberg's huge central graveyard and, after much rooting around, in a quiet corner I managed to find probably the most contentious memorial of them all, unnamed for obvious reasons but inscribed with a poem by Karl August Förster. Erich Mielke was head of the Stasi, the hated East German state security force and equivalent to the Soviet Union's KGB, which spied on and tortured its own people. The Stasi was, in fact, based here in Lichtenberg too, with the old headquarters in Normannenstrasse occupied now by a fabulous museum documenting the methods occupied by the Stasi to control the population. Mielke's old office is left untouched from the day it was vacated, a superb yet sinister time capsule of a different era.

There exists a strange nostalgia in some quarters for the old East Germany. Whilst I don't share that particular yearning for the past, this chapter is actually a bit of railway nostalgia as the sleeper service I was using to begin my trip no longer exists. I was testing it out for quality, as it was also part of a London to Vladivostok rail extravaganza, travelling all the way by train to the Sea of Japan from London via Berlin, Warsaw, Moscow and the epic Trans-Siberian Railway. The Trans-Siberian experience from Moscow onwards was on a private charter train with luxurious cabins and meals, but there weren't many rail options between London and Moscow. Would this one fit the bill?

In the bleak, dimly lit late October darkness I found a corner café for a falafel and a couple of bottles of beer for the journey, dodging the small group of teenaged skinheads kicking around on the corner, which some might also find nostalgic but fills me with the childhood dread of early 80s school bullies. This really was deepest East Berlin, far from the bright lights of the KuDamm or Unter den Linden. Nowadays several swish trains a day ply the route between central Berlin's Hauptbahnhof and Warsaw Centralna. Back then, a quieter suburban station in East Berlin's eerie forgotten hinterland was the start point of a night-time adventure eastwards.

Departing late evening I settled into my sleeper cabin of the Polish train. If you haven't had the experience, it wasn't dissimilar to my Swedish escapade - a single bed is made for you, a second one would fold out from the wall to make for a two-berth cabin. If the train had been busy there would have been a previously unknown occupant on the top bunk, but this time at least I had the cabin to myself. There's a sink by the window that covers as a table, a rack for your bags and limited hanging space. Facilities are at the end of the carriage. The guard's hidey-hole had one of those big urns you find for heating water on Eastern European trains.

There followed another rough night in a sleeper cabin. This was not my first attempt to sleep on a train, something I had also never managed to achieve on a coach or a plane. It was, however, my first visit to Poland and, well, I'm just too curious about my whereabouts to sleep. After I celebrated my entry into Poland leaving Frankfurt an der Oder with my last sip of beer, I watched the stations through the night as we passed in darkness, leaving the train bleary eyed in the early morning at Warsawa Centralna, a cold, concrete underground warren of Soviet architecture.

This was 1 November, All Saints Day. I was aware of this, as only some of my meetings had been possible, with several postponing to the following day. All Saints Day is a big deal in some countries and it was definitely a big deal in Catholic Poland. Even in Soviet times the public holiday, when people commemorate their saints, but also the souls of their deceased relatives, was important enough to retain, albeit renamed as 'Day of the Dead'.

By now a blasé traveller, I had decided to travel without Zloty and intended to change some Euro on arrival. Reaching Warsaw Central at around 6am on a freezing November morning, expecting a quieter than usual capital city on a public holiday, I was instead faced with nothing open at all. No bureau de change, no café, nothing. A public loo was available, but it was guarded by a fearsome looking elderly woman with a small bowl for loose change. It probably cost pence, but I didn't have a penny to spend and so crossed my legs. Looking at the thick creases in the lavatory attendant's face, etched into tough skin by a hard life cleaning ceramic and central European winters, I imagined she would take no prisoners. Isn't it strange how you need the loo more when it's cold?

I couldn't check into my hotel room at that unheard of time of day, so dropped off my bags, changed some money, spent that penny and found the one place open for breakfast in Warsaw on a public holiday...McDonalds! The McBreakfast menu hadn't reached that particular establishment by 2008, which meant I had to stomach a burger and fries to start the day. This just gets better, doesn't it? The glamorous lifestyle of the travel professional!

With my first meeting later that morning, this was my opportunity to sightsee. And what an unlikely opportunity. Early morning on the quietest, most solemn day of the year, Warsaw's Old Town was empty. I felt like I had it to myself, the vast open square, King Sigismund's Column and the Royal Castle. Whilst it feels like one of the great untouched medieval Old Towns of Europe, the truth is very different. In fact, the Old Town was virtually destroyed by the Nazis in 1944, an act of vengeance for the Warsaw Uprising by the Polish Resistance forces. With the war all but lost and the Red Army advancing fast, they razed Warsaw to the ground. The Soviets, on the other hand, deliberately sat back on the other side of the river and let the destruction take place, knowing they would then take a city and a people that had already been defeated. The Poles, through their geography, have suffered more than most at the hands of dictatorships.

The one very dominant Soviet building remaining looms large as soon as you leave Warsawa Centralna. The Palace of Culture is one of those bombastic buildings, very similar to one I saw in Riga, the Latvian Academy of Sciences. This kind of Stalinist architecture is referred to as Socialist Classicism and, even though they must be reminders of a dark period of their history, I am still glad they haven't been torn down. They are part of the power of history. That said, the Palace of Culture is so massive, if they tried to pull it down it would probably take half of central Warsaw with it.

Warsaw was well on the road to becoming a tourist destination, even back then, with western hotel chains firmly established and budget airlines serving the city from all over Europe. I enjoyed my couple of days in the city, after that inauspicious start. I like Polish food too. On the final evening I was invited out to dinner at a traditional restaurant by a potential supplier, which turned out to be an awkwardly romantic candlelit table for two. We had smalec for starters, basically dripping on toast to us Yorkshire folk. Hey, maybe he had done his homework on Yorkshire and was determined to show me a good time.

'Is that the time? Well, thanks for dinner but, erm, I have an early morning train to catch. I'll be in touch.'

My train to Krakow didn't depart from the rabbit warren maze of Warsaw Centralna. Instead, I would have to make my way to Zachodnia, the city's west station. It was a fair walk, but I fancied the fresh air. It's a fair distance too, a good couple of miles at least along one of those big wide arteries favoured by the old Eastern Bloc regimes when they rebuilt after World War II. There wasn't much fresh air, but finally I arrived at a building with Zachodnia written on it.

Nowhere was a departure to Krakow mentioned on the screens, so with maybe twenty minutes to wait until departure I queued up at a ticket counter. When my turn finally arrived it was abruptly pointed out to me that this was the bus station! I legged it in the direction the lady was gesticulating towards. At the train station there was no working departure board, no information desk. I legged it again, this time onto each platform, my case in tow, only to find no indication on the platform either of where any train might be heading. Asking around in English whether anyone could help, with flummoxed responses all around me and now a couple of minutes before the scheduled departure, a chap saw my German Tourist Board sponsored satchel, took pity on me and pointed to the correct platform in German. Dzięki! Danke! Thank you!

The old school PKP Polish Inter City train from Warsaw to Krakow back then afforded compartment-style carriages and a complimentary cup of coffee during the journey. On arrival in Krakow, some four to five hours later, I was met by a smattering of snow and an affable guide who showed me what I needed to see, the alternative hotels to the one we had brochured, plus the honeypot, the city's core. The Sukiennice or Cloth Hall is the centrepiece of the Rynek Główny or Market Square, the largest in medieval square in Europe and part of Krakow's UNESCO World Heritage site.

In the depths of a large hotel I did a deal that kept our business with our loyal supplier at a price they could live with too. With nobody hurt I went to have dinner at the restaurant that our customers experienced in the Kazimierz District or Jewish Quarter. But it was hard to eat in a Jewish restaurant in a quarter and city cleared decades ago of Jewish people and culture. One popular excursion from Krakow is Auschwitz, a place I would consider very important to visit personally, but at the same time I dread the selfie sticks of mass tourism at such a place for reflection. On a travel Facebook page recently a travel agent asked whether it was possible to feature Auschwitz and Chernobyl on the same trip. Well, you could kind of do it by train if you were prepared to rough it, but why would you consider that a holiday?

Each to their own. I'd highly recommend Warsaw and Krakow, great and contrasting cities. And I'd highly recommend travelling by train if you have time. From Berlin, on the lovely express daytime services from Hauptbahnhof that have replaced my night train to Warsaw.

Chapter 6 - The Hills are Alive

'We were disgusted with your choice of hotel in Vienna. My husband was shocked to see nearly naked ladies of the night gyrating and gesticulating at him from shop windows. How would you like to stay in a red light district?' wrote Mrs Gusted from Diss.

Actually, they weren't the only customers complaining about the location of the hotel on the Gürtel (belt) main road opposite Westbahnhof station. I would be in Vienna anyway for the Austrian Tourist Board's event and so decided to head off early to investigate. The following evening, after a day scouring Vienna for viable alternatives to the company's long-standing hotel in, according to some customers at least, the arse-end of Europe's worst den of iniquity, there would be a bit of culture. But first, following an evening arrival and with my female colleague safely in her room, I did my duty.

The customary walk around the block. I do it everywhere, just to make sure I've not chosen somewhere unsafe or unsavoury for guests. I braced myself. This was the hotel chosen by the company's previous owners, convenient for the station, modern and very friendly, but what would I find round the corner? The answer was nothing out of the ordinary. I walked round the block once. Nothing. I walked round again just to make sure. Still nothing untoward. What was all the fuss about?

Relieved that we might not need to switch hotels after all and back at the main entrance on the main road, I spotted a red light in the distance across the very broad boulevard. Negotiating two lanes of traffic, a wide central reservation with tramlines running along it, then two more lanes of traffic, there eventually appeared a bar with a red light in the window, plus a woman in her undies on a stool. I figured that maybe we would need to look for an alternative after all. But I also figured that Mr Gusted from Diss must have been a very determined man in his effort to become aroused, I mean disgusted, willing to dodge four lanes of busy traffic as well as Vienna's tram system in order to protect Mrs Gusted from Diss from the seedy side of Vienna.

After a day scouring Vienna we headed out to Schönbrunn Palace, summer residence of the Habsburg royals, where we enjoyed a classical music concert of the Viennese greats, Strauss and Mozart. Now that's what the stereotypical Vienna is all about, surely. I had been a couple of times before and wanted to show my colleague the palace's back garden, a stunning formal park leading uphill to the Gloriette monument. Wandering outside in winter evening darkness, illuminated by palace lights, we heard the ominous clunk of the door locking behind us. Lights then began to be switched off and it seemed likely that our nice hotel in a busy part of Vienna (or crack den in the middle of a brothel, according to Mr & Mrs Gusted from Diss) would be substituted for a bench in the grounds of a former royal palace. We frantically began trying any door handle we could find until finally one worked, taking us into the backstage dressing rooms, the band in their underwear, changing from period costume to normal clothes after the gig. I hope we waltzed through unnoticed.

My flight home was booked from Salzburg a few days after the travel show, but I had decided to take a risk and do something freestyle, something spontaneous. For the days between the show and the flight I had no accommodation arranged and no pre-planned idea where I would go. I had decided to see what took my fancy at the show, cadge a freebie or two and then head off out into the unknown to find something new and exciting.

St Pölten, my first stop, isn't the most exciting town in Europe, despite being state capital of Lower Austria. I was only there for the trains. St Pölten, you see, is the start point of the Mariazellerbahn Railway, a narrow-gauge route operated with electric power by the local federal government transport provider, climbing through what could be described as mountains in Lower Austria to the pilgrimage village of Mariazell in neighbouring Styria. They were a really friendly bunch at the trade show and, with the train being virtually empty amidst the winter smattering of snow down the valley bottom, they pretty much insisted that I ride up to Mariazell in the driver's cab.

Mariazell was an important destination for pilgrims in Habsburg times and this railway can definitely be described as a journey, stretching 85 km from St Pölten to the mountain village via multiple tunnels, bridges and viaducts. The first section crosses flat terrain before rolling through the hilly pastures of the Pielach Valley, climbing gradually through what's known as the 'Talstrecke' or 'Valley Route'. Passing through the Weissenburgtunnel into the narrower Nattersbach Valley, from Laubenbachmühle the mountain section begins. Over the next 20 km the railway has plenty of tricks up its sleeve, with a double horseshoe curve and the longest tunnel on the line, the Gösingtunnel at nearly 2 ½ km in length, which also marks the highest point on the Mariazellerbahn at nearly 900m above sea level. The smattering of snow now noticeably deeper, the railway crosses viaducts, passes lakes, follows wooded gorges towered over by rocky crags in a scene of wild beauty.

At line's end, Mariazell station is about a kilometre from the village. Sometimes a steam tramway connects the two, but my only option was to trudge merrily through the deep snow in the sunshine. Before I reached the basilica and my hotel visit I couldn't resist climbing a little higher, the local tourist board escorting me to the Bürgeralpe ski station at 1267m on the Mariazeller Schwebebahn cable car, which has survived the threat of closure many times since the resort's heyday. Back in the village, my hotel was on 'Ruhetag' or quiet day, closed to the public, a quaint tradition at family-run establishments giving themselves and colleagues a midweek breather. They showed me round their charming Gasthaus, set on an equally charming square opposite the basilica that dominates Mariazell. Forgetting the cold for a moment, you could imagine a glorious summer's day here, sipping a coffee and devouring a strudel amidst the pilgrims, both railway pilgrims and religious ones. Speaking of which, the basilica itself, also known as the

Basilica of the Birth of the Virgin Mary, with its central Gothic tower flanked by twin baroque towers, is Austria's most important destination for pilgrims.

Next stop Salzkammergut. If you don't know it, the holiday region is often called the Austrian Lake District in the UK, a traditional and very popular destination east of Salzburg, the 'Sound of Music' city. With its own 'Sound of Music' connections (the wedding scene in the movie was filmed at Mondsee in the Salzkammergut) as well as the ubiquitous Mozart (whose mother was born in St Gilgen and, blimey, don't they let you know it!), the Austrian Lakes had somehow failed to reach the radar of my employer. Which is surprising as a fabulously scenic regional railway runs right through the heart of it.

An InterCity train whizzed me from St Pölten through Lower Austria, through the Danube city of Linz to a little known junction town called Attnang-Puchheim. From here the conveniently named Salzkammergutbahn runs to another little-known town called Stainach-Irdning. Thankfully there is an incredible amount of interest in between these nondescript junction villages. Moving swiftly on from the sniggersome first stop called Wankham, things get really interesting at Gmunden, the main town at the north end of Traunsee lake.

Gmunden railway station sits above the town and lake, too far to walk in normal circumstances but even more so with two feet of snow on the ground. There is no need to worry though as outside the station you can catch the Gmunden Tramway, operated by Stern & Hafferl, who built the line in 1894. It's the oldest and shortest tramway in Austria, as well as one of the steepest in the world, trundling 2 ½ km to the head of my favourite Salzkammergut lake, Traunsee.

The tramway has been extended recently to connect with Stern & Hafferl's Traunseebahn service, a private heritage railway, but still more of a commuter service than a tourist train, connecting Gmunden with the farming villages of its hinterland. Although the Traunseebahn is more one for the enthusiasts, it is still a pleasant enough half hour ride up to Vorchdorf, the most interesting stop being Schloss Eggenberg near the end of the line, a private brewery since 1681 and, before the advent of the craft beer revolution, the brewer of the world's strongest beer.

My hotel for the night would be a family-run Gasthaus in the village of Traunkirchen. The hotelier picked me up at Traunkirchen station, which was too far from his hotel for most people to walk, particularly with a case in tow. It's a regular dilemma. Whilst it would be great to always feature a hotel across from the railway station, sometimes it just isn't possible and road transfers are required. My quandary here was further amplified by the fact that there is a second station in the village, closer to the centre and hotel, named Traunkirchen Ort. It is actually more a halt than a station and, having walked up and down the hill between hotel and Traunkirchen Ort station a couple of times, pondering both the distance and the incline, ultimately it would still need a transfer. I am glad I trudged up there through the snow for the view over Traunkirchen, with its promontory jutting out into the most fjord-like lake in the Salzkammergut, the headland crowned by the simple parish church, the surrounding mountains dressed in crisp, white winter coat. If it hadn't been so cold, with darkness setting in too, I could have stayed up there longer, mesmerised by today's new favourite place.

At the village of Ebensee the lake disappears, the Salzkammergutbahn heading through countryside to the region's main town, Bad Ischl, once a favoured spa of the Habsburg monarchy. I sneaked away from the train here, hopping on a bus to Strobl on the southern shore of Wolfgangsee or Lake Wolfgang. A boat would gently sail me across the icy blue water to St Wolfgang itself, a village with a rail highlight of its own.

Austria's steepest cog railway, the Schafbergbahn, begins its rise in St Wolfgang. The journey to the top takes just over half an hour, covering nearly 6km of track. Riding through the forests there are eventually superb views of Lake Wolfgang as you finally climb above the treeline, with the train disappearing through tunnels engineered in hostile mountain terrain to reach the mountain station, some 1,732 metres above sea level. Blessed once again with a crisp day, the views are heavenly.

Back on the Salzkammergutbahn, heading south through the pastures of the valley bottom, soon the final highlight emerges, one of Austria's most photographed villages. Hallstatt sits dreamily perched on the cliff-side shore of its own lake, a simple church spire as its focal point and the steep Dachstein massif as a backdrop. There is a halt rather than a station named Hallstatt, however, please don't request it unless you have arranged an onward transfer. The station, you see, lies across the lake from the village, accessed by boat. When our groups would visit on a day excursion this is exactly what they would do, sailing towards the honeypot village of the region, drinking every last drop of the photogenic scene that has graced a thousand holiday brochure front covers. How do you follow that?

By exploring those mountains beyond the village, I guess, would be the only way. The salz in Salzkammergut refers to salt. The Hallstatt and Dachstein region has many attractions, one of which is the world's oldest salt mine. On another glorious day I opted for another rail journey of sorts. The Dachstein-Krippenstein cable cars, whisked me from Obertraun in the valley, a mere 600 metres above sea level, to Schönbergalm (1,340 metres), then the local mountain, Krippenstein (2069 metres). Austria might not have as many mountain railways as its near neighbour, Switzerland, but hills were alive for me, the cogs whirring on the rails and also in my mind. It is such a satisfying feeling, searching into the unknown, happening on something so special, then sharing it with others.

Chapter 7 - Murder, Steam and Clotted Cream

L et's start this chapter departing Exeter. After completing the grand tour of Scotland I was planning a second UK tour and the first English one. The company had built its name in the Eurostar era, trailblazing group travel by train to the Continent, but these were the first steps in producing a UK programme, with the credit crunch hitting hard and some customers looking closer to home for holidays. That Scottish round trip had been a hit, so we needed a wider programme and quick.

With two young children at home, Mrs C having called a break on her own career to look after them full-time, I avoided being away at weekends. I would be visiting as many hotels as possible in Devon and Cornwall in five days, shoe-horning a couple of steam trains in where I could, before flying back from Newquay to Leeds on the Friday evening.

From Exeter city centre, the train famously hugs the Exe Estuary, before even more famously hitting the coast at Dawlish Warren, running right along the charming seafront of Regency resort Dawlish, where you can almost touch the sandcastles and smell the candy floss as you trundle past the sands and the coastal path.

A short detour inland courtesy of the Teign Estuary brings us to Newton Abbot, heading back to the seaside again at Torquay, whose station is somewhat out of town on the seafront, but conveniently just across the road from the hotel I was hoping would fit our groups, the Grand.

The Grand Hotel is the place where Agatha Christie spent her honeymoon night with her first husband, Archie, on Christmas Eve 1914. Archie was serving with the Royal Flying Corps and had come home on leave from France. Nowadays the author's name lives large across the Torbay region and from the hotel you can walk the 'Agatha Christie Mile' along the promenade to Torquay's other elegant landmark Victorian hotel with Christie connections, the Imperial Hotel, where she attended many functions in her youth and would later set several of her novels.

Having dropped my bags in my room at the Grand I ventured out for the evening. Tantalisingly just across the road is the Kings Bowls Club, setting for the 2003 film 'Blackball' with Paul Kaye, Johnny Vegas and Bernard Cribbins cast within a mixed plot about a bad-boy bowler from the wrong side of the tracks trying to make his way up a game entrenched in polite applause, tea and cucumber sandwiches.

With a packed following day, visiting three 4* hotels in Torquay, a couple of hotels in Paignton, plus a steam excursion, this was my only chance to get a feel for the rest of Torquay's accommodation options. It was interesting to see which coaches were parked outside the various hotels and, as the evening went on, to hear the live entertainment obligatory at traditional seaside group hotels booming from the ballrooms and bars, more often than not a singalong to 'Hi Ho Silver Lining'.

Hopping on a train in Torquay five minutes later you arrive in Paignton, a traditional seaside town of fish & chips, sticks of rock and kiss me quick nostalgia. But the nostalgia doesn't stop there. The Paignton & Dartmouth Steam Railway operates from Paignton station along a preserved part of the former Great Western network to Dartmouth, as the name suggests, although Dartmouth is reached at the end using a ferry service across the Dart Estuary from Kingswear, which can be included in the ticket.

Having had a good look around Paignton, my overriding memory is of someone sunbathing on the pavement in the main shopping street. And I do mean just sprawled out next to the kerb, lying on the tarmac, catching the sun's rays, with tourists stepping over to put their chip wrappers in the bin. No, actually, that aside, it's a pleasant enough town with a great beach and promenade, lots of green space and some nice hotels too.

The good people at the Paignton & Dartmouth Steam Railway showed me their preserved 'First Class' wagon with some pride, a Pullman observation car made for the 'Devon Belle' service that once graced the route from Paddington to Paignton in luxury in the golden age. The period carriage would be hooked to the rear of the train for the best views. At this point I would normally be telling you to sit on either the left or right hand side of the carriage, but this one is pretty impossible to call. It's a journey of two very different halves.

From Paignton the glorious scenery for the first half of the journey begins immediately on the left hand side, with seascapes and vast sandy Torbay beaches as you trundle above the charming, colourful beach huts of Goodrington Sands. The drama of a steam train, coupled with the innocent pleasures of the Devon seaside could grace any poem by Betjeman, that loquacious lover of the southwest and the railways. Hopefully there wouldn't be any sand in the sandwiches and wasps in the tea today though.

I did say this was a journey of two halves. That's because, after Greenway Halt (where you could hop off to explore Agatha Christie's Greenway Estate) things eventually switch from the coastal panoramas of the left to the serene glistening waters of the River Dart's estuary on the right, with boats bobbing in the harbours and delightful Dartmouth, with its naval college, just across the water. A short foot passenger ferry whisks you from Kingswear to Dartmouth itself for a well-earned pint in the sunshine. Well, that's what I did anyway!

Leaving Torquay the following morning to begin planning the Cornish part of the eventual tour, I had one final thing to do before leaving the 'English Riviera'. From Totnes station it's a pleasant enough 500 yard walk along the paths to Totnes Riverside station, one of the termini of the South Devon Railway, another jigsaw piece of the preserved sections of the Great Western Railway, a branch line built in 1872, closed to passengers since 1958, but saved for future generations. The South Devon Railway has operated a scenic steam and diesel railway for tourists through the scenic Dart Valley between Totnes and Buckfastleigh since 1969.

After chatting with the volunteers at Totnes, most of whom were very interested in the purpose of my visit as they were regular customers of the company I was representing, we departed Totnes on the seven mile route, recreating the glory pre-war days of the GWR.

First point of interest is the Royal Mile. Apparently here they used to stable the Royal trains bound for Dartmouth Naval College. From here we join the beautiful valley of the River Dart, which flirts in and out of view as the loco gently chuffs through the woodland through Staverton and onwards to Buckfastleigh, where the railway has an excellent museum in its old engine sheds and refreshment rooms. For passengers with more time to spare than I had, Dartmoor Otters and Buckfast Butterflies are nearby attractions to make a full day out in bonny Buckfastleigh.

Back in Totnes and onto the mainline heading westwards through Devon towards Cornwall, the next point of major interest actually spans those two counties. Literally. The Royal Albert Bridge is an icon of the Victorian age of engineering and, designed by Isambard Kingdom Brunel, was opened in 1859 by Victoria's consort, Prince Albert. It still carries the Cornish mainline from Plymouth to Saltash across the Tamar.

Lostwithiel, Par, St Austell, the names begin to trip off the tongue, memories of a childhood holiday a long long way from Yorkshire, before Britain's southernmost city, Truro, with its impressive cathedral looms into view on the left from the train's vantage point. From Truro I changed onto the first of our Cornish branch lines, the Maritime Line, which descends through a green, rural idyll, via charming little Cornish towns like Penryn on its way to the sea at Falmouth, a maritime port and resort that boasts two stations, Falmouth Town and Falmouth Docks. I decided to drag my bag around the town for a while before taking a taxi to my next hotel visit, facing the prom and Castle Beach.

'The Royal Duchy?' said the taxi driver, 'That'll be the best address in town!'

The meeting went well. It was, and still is, a smashing hotel, the Duchy. I needn't have looked further but prefer to cover all options.

The next hotel that afternoon, after leaving the Duchy, was to the right along the prom around the bay. The Falmouth Beach Hotel made the news a few of years later in 2012 when it was tragically destroyed in a terrible fire, with guests at the time including the guitarist from Blur.

Such a terrible shame as it was such a nice welcoming hotel, although I was by now running late, clock-watching and so the meeting came and went in a bit of a…erm…blur. True, it was no country house, unlike the Duchy, but it was soon to go bang, there's no other way to describe it, boys and girls.

'Is this your level now? Making sentences up using Blur songs?' I can hear you say. 'This is a low! You charmless man!'

So, having visited the Duchy and the Falmouth Beach, but late for my final meeting of the day, I stumbled out of the Falmouth Beach Hotel onto the promenade. Concerned. I hate being late. The last hotel was the Falmouth Hotel. Did I mention yet that I was late? Oh, and I didn't know where the hell the Falmouth Hotel was. Panic was beginning to set in. Would I get there before the Sales Manager clocked off for the day?

Thankfully, a figure I vaguely recognised was walking along the promenade in my direction. As he approached I could see from his swagger that it was the lead singer of the 1980 pop reggae group, Musical Youth. I wondered whether he could help. After all, he had bagged a number one hit single at the age of 15. And then there was also the Grammy Awards nomination. Impressive stuff.

'Excuse me, sir. Could you tell me where the Falmouth Hotel is please?'

The former number one record producing, Grammy Award nominated child prodigy stopped, pondered, then pointed towards a building in the distance around the bay.

'Pass the Duchy, pon the left hand side.'

Maybe this didn't actually happen. Maybe I made it up. Okay, it's actually my one and only hotel contractor joke and I may have used it many times. If it made you chuckle, thank you. You are possibly the first person not to hold their head in their hands. Thanks also to Musical Youth and goodnight everyone. Tomorrow would be another day.

At that stage I didn't know where I would be staying the following night, the final night of my trip. I had left this in the capable hands of Anne in the office, our admin whizz who used to turn the gobbledygook I would squawk at a voice recorder into trip reports. It later transpired that she had found me a bed in a B&B in Newlyn, just round the bay from Penzance, so off I trotted on one last day's exploring Cornwall's branch lines.

Back along the Maritime Line I went from Falmouth Docks to Truro, joining the mainline again westwards towards Penzance, the end of the line and the end of England station-wise. I had one final detour to make first though. After passing Redruth and Camborne I reached St Erth, a junction station with access to the St Ives Bay branch line, which is short but most definitely sweet. Make sure you sit on the right hand side, folks, and get yourselves ready for the immediate pleasures of spectacular Carbis Bay, with a coastline of golden sands to warm your soul. In just ten minutes the train trundles into St Ives, with beaches, harbour, boats, quaint shops and art galleries. There are few places more pleasant.

Back up the line to St Erth to rejoin the mainline, the train trundled along the final ten minutes of track into Penzance, the last station in England, but not before allowing more than a fleeting glimpse of mysterious St Michael's Mount offshore on the left hand side, a great end to the day. Well, not quite the end of the day, as I made my way to Newlyn and my B&B.

'Would you write something in my guest book?'

I had only just arrived and plonked my bags in the hall. Why would I want to write in her guest book? I hadn't even seen my room. Hell, I hadn't even been given my key yet. What did she want me to put? 'B&B with overbearing landlady and public areas bursting with trinkets and general crazy crap nightmare commemorative ornaments bought from Sunday newspaper pull-out magazine adverts'? The equally crazy Cornish landlady's rule seemed to be, 'Write in my guest book, then you get your room key!' so I wrote something bland in her blasted guest book.

She wanted to know everything, about why I was in Newlyn for one night, but didn't read the signs that I was at the end of my working day, just wanted a pub meal and a pint by the harbour, then forty winks. I was a long way from home. Just about as far away as it was possible to be on the mainland, as it happens. I was missing my girls. I just needed the room key that was still firmly in her grasp. Having been given a lengthy briefing about everything I could do in Newlyn, Mousehole and Penzance, had I not been staying just the one night with work, still the key remained elusive. Having been recommended a local 'medieval night', where you are served mead, whose door I had no intention of darkening (though I nodded politely anyway, giving the impression I'd consider it), finally the room key was mine. Oh, for the easy come, easy go anonymity of a hotel room.

The following morning, with Penzance's small selection of hotels ruled out for one reason or another, I began my journey home. I had decided to fly from Newquay to Leeds Bradford for ease and so rejoined the Cornish mainline at Penzance, retracing my tracks as far as Par, before switching to the branch line marketed as the "Atlantic Coast Line" to Newquay, a coast to coast journey in its own right.

Par brought back memories of a childhood holiday in Cornwall. My parents had just got into caravanning and hitched their new (well, second hand but it was new to them) caravan to the back of the car, completely underestimating how far Cornwall is from Yorkshire. The following week was punctuated with statements like, 'We've got better scenery in Yorkshire,' or 'It's not as nice as Whitby.' I seem to recall we came home early, so disillusioned were they with the delights of the Duchy. Amidst all this, Par was the saving grace as it was the one beach where dogs were allowed. A beach with a power station at the end of it, if my memory serves me correctly.

From Par the Atlantic Coast Line trundles through the Luxulyan Valley and across Goss Moor, with visible traces of tin mining history amidst the pleasant, if not spectacular, scenery. The Atlantic comes into view, but there would be too little time to sample many of Newquay's pleasures. The beaches, the waves, the seafood, Newquay has something for everyone. There was an interesting mix of school parties, surfers, senior coach groups and also some stags and hens arriving for the weekend. The weekend was here for me too. In no time the wonders of aviation would transport me back to the beloved old Yorkshire my parents had craved whilst in Cornwall, more so the beloved family I so missed during my weeks away. The wonders of aviation then went missing, with hours of delay and a re-routing to East Midlands. I could have got home quicker in dad's crawling, caravan-towing, road-clogging car! But I really wish I'd taken the train instead. A lesson learned.

Chapter 8 - The Tracks of Deep South USA

'**A**h laayeft mah keys eeen mah caarrr,' said Jay in his gentle southern drawl.

We were at the beginning of a circular tour that would take in Atlanta, Chattanooga, Nashville, Memphis, New Orleans and back to Atlanta, all within eight days to put together a new tour combining the great musical cities and railroads of Deep South USA. Jay was my local guide for the trip, Sales Director of the local company that would help me make it work. A big guy with a big heart and gentle nature, Jay was the perfect companion and interesting company, adding great insight and the occasional bit of local flavour I would have otherwise missed. I would wager Jay was in his mid-60s at the time of our journey, which meant that he would have known the Deep South prior to the rise of the Civil Rights Movement, as well as living through times of great upheaval and change. That first morning we had visited Margaret Mitchell House, commemorating the author of 'Gone with the Wind' and we had just spent half an hour or so at a curio called Cyclorama, a huge cylindrical painting depicting the Battle of Atlanta during the Civil War. The plan had been to get on the road to our next stop, Chattanooga, but we were destined to spend longer in the Cyclorama car park than in Cyclorama itself waiting for a locksmith. Thankfully, we'd had a decent breakfast of Southern specialities that would follow us around the tour – grits, biscuits and gravy. Imagine a type of scone with white sauce poured over it and a side dish of polenta.

That's the closest I can get to describing my first Deep South breakfast and, well, when in Rome!

The locksmith arrived to find a way into Jay's car. He knew what he was doing, this dude. Watching him break the lock you got the feeling that he had taken a lifelong hobby and turned it into a reputable profession. That aside, we were grateful to be back on the road and bound for the first leg of our roadtrip.

Pardon me boy, is that the Chattanooga Choo Choo

I've stayed in hundreds of hotels and been shown around hundreds more. Hotel rooms tend to have pretty much the same stuff in them and you would think it would be impossible by now to get excited about a hotel. Then once in a while along comes a special one. There was nothing particularly special about the rooms at the Chattanooga Choo Choo Hotel. They were functional, set within a number of modern blocks attached to the main historic building. In fact, at the time of our visit I thought some of the rooms probably were in need of a little attention (and they've had a refurbishment since, I might add!), but it was everything else that made the hotel special.

Pardon me boy, but there is no track 29 anymore. For a country built on rail, the US passenger rail system has shrunk dramatically to a few long-distance lines and commuter services during decades where road and air travel usurped rail to the point where most Americans won't consider rail travel an option. I once had a conversation with a representative of Dallas Tourism who swore blind that Dallas did not have an AMTRAK train station (it does), that there was no rail link to her city (there is) and that nobody in the USA travels by train (erm, she had a point there). No choo choos have steamed into Chattanooga for a long time, but Chattanooga Terminal Station was saved from the wrecking ball in 1973, reopening as a hotel and visitor experience. The hotel reception is the former ticket office, set within a rather grand booking hall. Out back between what was the station building and the accommodation blocks are tracks on which are positioned Pullman sleeper carriages that can be booked for a supplement, plus a model railway and a restaurant with singing waiters. The electric bus terminal is situated next to the hotel, offering free, green transportation to downtown Chattanooga within minutes. What's not to like, I ask you?

There are still working tracks around Chattanooga, thanks to the Tennessee Valley Railroad Museum, whose volunteers first stored, then restored locomotives on site since the 1960s and who built a line on which to run heritage rail excursions. From the railroad's Grand Junction station, the six mile round trip chugs across the Chickamauga Creek, through the 986 feet long Missionary Ridge Tunnel to the railroad's sheds, the engines spinning on a turntable before making the return journey. They had clearly been warned about the arrival of a geeky Brit (who, me?!) as the train ran just for me that day, plus they let me sit in the cab with the driver, also kindly opening the engine sheds so I could get a whiff of the grease and rust of restoration in progress.

Across town is another track of note. From St Elmo station the Lookout Mountain Incline Railroad describes itself as 'America's Most Amazing Mile'. The current funicular was built way back in 1895 as a tourist railway to link Chattanooga with Lookout Mountain, a significant Civil War site where raged the "battle above the clouds". With the steepest incline at 72.7%, it's certainly a ride with a difference, with great views and attractions at the top enabling you to while away a few hours. We didn't have hours to while away though. Jay was waiting for me at the top, ready for the next leg of our road trip, heading through Tennessee to Lynchburg.

Lynchburg. The name might ring a bell with a few of you? It has stared across the bar at me on many occasions, sometimes in good focus, sometimes not so. Yes, Lynchburg is home to Jack Daniel's Distillery. We enjoyed an informative tour with a really engaging guide, explaining how the distillery makes its own charcoal and crafts its own barrels, which differentiates JD from its competitors. Only one thing was missing from the tour and that was a tasting of the fine spirit itself, as Lynchburg is in a dry county. Sod's Law, I believe that since then they've somehow started doing tours including a tasting, but that day I had to make do with a thirst-quenching homemade lemonade. Cheers! Let's get back on the road, Jay!

Nashville

Next stop Nashville. I'm sure those words have been uttered by many a musician, dreaming of a big break at the home of Country Music, the Grand Ole Opry, live music venues and recording studios galore. I can't play a note, nor have I ever been particularly interested in Country Music, but the anticipation grew as we approached the city by car. We wouldn't get there straight away though as my guide, Jay, who was driving me between cities no longer connected by train, had arranged a first visit to 'Opryland Resort & Convention Center' on the outskirts of town. It was an underwhelming start to discover that the Grand Ole Opry had moved from the historic Ryman Auditorium building in the centre of Nashville to a purpose-built entertainment complex on the edge of the city, complete with resort hotel and shopping mall, but as darkness began to fall I promised myself a couple of evening hours exploring the real Nashville and a Jack Daniel's or two to compensate for Lynchburg's lemonade.

And what a city! For any music lover, irrespective of genre. Okay, I'm not into Country as such, but you can't deny that a place has a particular aura and significant history. Plus, I quite like the band Big Star who also came out of Nashville in the 1970s. A short walk from my hotel took me past the beautiful Ryman Auditorium, the home of the Grand Ole Opry from the 1920s until the 1970s, and down Broadway, the antithesis of the usual US downtown. Most American city centres empty after workers have left for home, leaving behind an eerie atmosphere that can even be a tad foreboding, but Broadway by contrast is lined either side with lively honky tonk bars, with live music blasting out from every one. I hopped from bar to bar, listening to talented musicians playing Country Music of all types for the occasional dollar thrown into their tip buckets, imagining that for every one of those bands and musicians who had 'made it' onto Broadway, there must be hundreds more aspiring to tread those stages.

The next morning I met Jay for breakfast. Grits were probably consumed, along with biscuit and gravy. You know the score by now. Before leaving Nashville on our whistle stop route by road through Tennessee to finally connect with the AMTRAK rail system, we would have one final visit to make, to the Country Music Hall of Fame. Well, I think I might have mentioned that I'm not a Country Music fan, but I am most certainly a music fan, and any music fan could spend the whole day there, tracing the music's tracks from the rural backwaters to the Nashville charts. The Sales Director of the museum, Keith, was an instantly likeable and funny character. Surrounded by the good and the great of Country Music, from Hank Williams through to Johnny Cash and onwards to the modern era, when Keith asked me who I was into I proudly suggested my one and only Country Music choice as a lifeline. Laura Cantrell is a recording artist from Nashville who, thanks to the dedication of the late great John Peel, who played her music endlessly on his Radio 1 shows around the turn of the last century, probably has a more passionate fanbase in the UK than in Tennessee as a result. If you haven't heard her sing, her voice has textures from which emanate emotion and power that give me goosebumps. Keith was impressed by my answer, but blew me away with his own music of choice. Yes, the boss of the Country Music Hall of Fame told me, 'I like Country Music, but my all-time favourite artist is Cilla Black.' Before I could respond with, 'Surprise surprise, the unexpected hits you between the eyes!' Keith had moved on with a brilliant suggestion. 'Would you like to see Studio B? Your groups can visit there too. It will be a great combination with the Country Music Hall of Fame.'

Entering RCA Studio B, the corridor is lined with photographs of eminent singers and musicians famed the world over, who all clearly recorded in this outwardly unassuming building. There's Roy Orbison, Jim Reeves too, oh and Charley Pride, my late mother's favourite singer. Elvis looms large. So does Dolly Parton. And the Everly Brothers. Wow, the list goes on. It's the music that was force-fed to me by my parents at home and in their car through my childhood in the 1970s and early 80s and against which I suppose I was bound to rebel. From the corridor we entered a darkened room, Keith, Jay and I, with excerpts from the greatest Studio B recordings gently cascading from the speakers, after which the room was illuminated to reveal that we were standing in the famous recording studio itself, an impressive experience for any music fan touring Nashville's sights. The lights revealed much more to my companions though, as I was overwhelmed and in tears. My lovely mum had passed away the previous year. At the crematorium my dad chose an Everly Brothers song that was dear to both of them to begin the service, plus her favourite song, 'Crystal Chandeliers' by Charley Pride, to accompany our final farewell. It had occurred to me during those couple of minutes of music in the darkness at a chance and unplanned extra visit that I was standing in the room where both of those songs were recorded. Cynics often accuse the USA of lacking culture or history, but I will treasure those moments, however sad, where Nashville culture and history collided with my own life and emotions. I'm a lucky man indeed.

I'm goin' to Jackson

When my boss broke the news to me that I would be looking after the company's American programme my heart sank. The USA programme mainly consisted of one amazing but lumbering monster of a tour series, trailing coast to coast from New York to San Francisco via DC, Chicago, Colorado, Arizona and LA, piecing together three overnight rail journeys with nine hotels. Forty times. Every year.

It was the dreaded task. Besides, the USA had never really been a holiday destination that had captured my imagination. There was so much of Europe for me to discover, where language and culture changes every few hours of your journey. Travel broadens the mind, thankfully, and all that was about to change as I experienced the hospitality of Americans.

The scenery of the road journey between Nashville and Memphis is hard to describe. The only emotions I can recall relate to fear and dread. Driving rain like I have never seen before lashed the windscreen of Jay's car. Visibility was zero. The big guy stoically grumbled a bit about the rain, but cheerily carried on driving into the abyss, hopefully unaware of my white knuckles gripping the seat, flashing before my eyes the images of the beautiful wife and daughters I would leave behind. This was a rock 'n' roll road trip but, hell, did we have to pay homage to Eddie Cochran or Marc Bolan by going the same way?

The rain ceased. We were still on time, thanks to Jay, who has since admitted to me that he was scared out of his brains too. Our next comfort stop was the curious Casey Jones Village. It's in Jackson, Tennessee, where the railroad engineer who died at the brake of his runaway train called home. The 'Ballad of Casey Jones' helped immortalise John Luther Jones and the 'village' named after him features a small railroad museum and outlet shopping. Only in America would such a tale develop into a retail opportunity and mini-theme park, but whilst I browsed the trinkets Jay disappeared, returning with the local speciality, cracklin' cornbread. Yum.

There are many towns named Jackson in the States. This one is also notable as the Jackson Johnny Cash and June Carter sang about and was also the home of Rockabilly king Carl Perkins of Blue Suede Shoes fame. But all that probably pales into insignificance by the next stop, Tupelo. Jay drove me past the Tupelo Hardware Company Store in downtown. It was here in January 1946 that a mother brought her son to buy his birthday present. It is said that the boy would have preferred a rifle, but Gladys Presley managed to persuade him to take a guitar instead. The rest, as they say, is history.

The Elvis Presley Birthplace Museum in Tupelo is authentic and inauthentic at the same time, but a fabulous place to visit. The two room wooden 'shotgun' house in which the Presleys brought up young Elvis, built by his father, grandfather and uncle, still stands as testament to the humble beginnings of the King of Rock n Roll. Another proud wooden building, the Assembly of God Pentecostal Church, stands close by and is the actual building where the Presleys worshipped, although it soon became clear that the building had been transported from a different place to this convenient spot for tourism purposes. Whilst I'm still contemplating whether that's right or not, there's no doubt that once inside the building, watching a floor to ceiling film of young Elvis letting go at service, it was a powerful introduction to what was to follow. Memphis.

Thank you. Thank you very much.

Letter to Memphis

We finally arrived in Memphis, Tennessee, Jay's hometown, the weekend about to start and a packed itinerary ahead of us. As we drove into the city down Union Avenue Jay pointed out a building on the right hand side with a guitar hanging from it and said we'd come back for a proper look the following day. It was Sun Studio. After checking out a few hotels we settled into our chosen lodging, just a couple of blocks from Beale St. Saturday would turn into a mindblowing day for me, but for now Jay's working week would end at a venue of his choice.

Charlie Vergos began to barbeque in 1948. Down a little alley close to the Peabody Hotel stands his Rendezvous restaurant, serving dry rub southern comfort food that today still tempts the tastebuds of Memphians, the connoisseurs of all things grilled. Jay pointed out the frail restaurateur, son of Greek immigrants, who had resolutely stayed in downtown Memphis through turbulent times following the assassination of Martin Luther King on 4th April 1968, contributing to the regeneration of the downtown neighbourhood that now attracts so many visitors.

Saturday was pure pleasure, an early start beginning a few blocks further out of town down Union Avenue with the Sun Studio tour. That's the legendary Sun Studio, folks, the self-styled birthplace of Rock n Roll. Opened in 1950 by Sam Phillips, the studio claims to have cut the first Rock n Roll record back in 1951. Then an 18 year old walked into the studio in 1953 to record a couple of songs as a gift for his mother. The boy Elvis would eventually make the studio its name and fortune, becoming the biggest musical phenomenon on the planet and this success fuelled the label's growing roster, at one time featuring Jerry Lee Lewis, Johnny Cash, Roy Orbison, BB King and Carl Perkins. The guided tour was excellent, from Sun Records memorabilia through to the recording studio, our young guide demonstrating on her guitar how Johnny Cash would stick a dollar bill between his guitar strings to create the rhythm sound of a train (well, there had to be a train reference in here somewhere!). After the obligatory pic of yours truly clutching the studio microphone, trying not to pout like Elvis, we were whisked away across town for the next visit.

If I was excited by Sun Studio, well, the next visit left an even bigger impression. We headed towards South Memphis, East McLemore Avenue to be precise. If you are into Soul, then Stax is Memphis Soul, the Soul of the South even. Less poppy than Motown, the roster of Stax was no less impressive or prolific. Otis Redding, Sam & Dave, Isaac Hayes, Carla Thomas, the Staple Singers, the list goes on, all backed by the house band, Booker T & the MGs. Jay told me that, in an era of racial tension in Memphis and the South in general, not to mention racial segregation, the MGs and the wider Stax team had presented one small oasis where the colour of your skin did not matter. The Stax building itself is a rebuilt replica of the original, but the museum is no less fascinating and you leave in awe of the talent and sound that exploded from this unassuming South Memphis street.

Graceland was, well, Graceland. I expected an Elvis theme park and, yes, you can spend a whole day there looking at the King's car collection, his private jet, exhibits from his musical career and also his time in the military, as well as the house itself. We made do mainly with the mansion, more humble than I had imagined and an interesting time capsule of the life of someone who still visibly moves many people today, as witnessed with some of my fellow visitors overwhelmed by emotion, sobbing at the singer's gravestone (at that time) just over 30 years after his untimely death.

Before I could say, "Thank you, thank you very much," (have I used this joke yet?) it was time to depart. Jay took his well- deserved leave from me. It was Saturday afternoon, after all, and from now on I was on my own again. Often a lone traveller, I used to jokingly call myself 'Monorail'. Thankfully, I had just about enough time to get to the Peabody Hotel for the duck march.

'The duck what?' I hear you ask. Okay, here's how it goes. Since the 1930s the fountain in the lobby of the Memphis Peabody Hotel has been home to the Peabody ducks. Twice daily a spectacle takes place. A Master of Ceremonies rolls out a red carpet, regales the eager onlooking crowd with the history of the Peabody Ducks, after which it all goes a bit…erm…quackers as the little blighters jump out of their fountain onto the red carpet laid out for them, waddling their way to the elevator to the obvious delight of the crowd.

It was snowing outside now, something quite unusual for Memphis. Walking back to my own hotel in the early evening I crossed the intersection of Beale Street. Now Beale Street would normally be lively of a Saturday evening anyway, but this time it was lively in a different way. Outside the famous blues bars a massive joyous snowball fight was taking place. I joined in, of course, then went my merry meandering Memphis way, past BB King's, past the Gibson Guitar Factory, past WC Handy's ("Father of the Blues") House. What a city!

A couple of hours later I was back on Beale, soaking up the atmosphere amongst the happy revellers hopping from bar to bar, with the sound of Memphis music filling every room of every hostelry. I loved the relaxed atmosphere, with no objection to taking your beer in a plastic pint from one place to the next. I chose to perch myself on a tall barstool to listen to a Blues veteran do his thing from a small stage. Every few songs he would burst into a rendition of his most played tune, 'Tip the band. You gotta tip the band.' Whilst the band played on the maestro walked around the room with his tip bucket, asking audience members for a donation, also asking where they were from, then marching back onto the stage to pronounce, 'All the way from Birmingham, Alabama!'

Finally, it was my turn. 'Where you from, man?' asked the singer. The cogs whirred in my brain. Rotherham, South Yorkshire? I doubt he has heard of Rotherham. Should I say Sheffield or Leeds? But will he have heard of those places either? I decided on my answer, then muttered it to him in embarrassment. He excitedly ran back onto the stage and pronounced, 'All the way from London, England!!!' I got a standing ovation from the rest of the bar for being transatlantic, if not particularly honest on this occasion, deciding it was time to wander through a doorway into the adjoining bar.

Into another world. The bigger adjoining bar was packed with people with broad smiles on their faces. This was a happy room, there was no question about that. On stage was a band with the usual drummer, bassist and guitarist, but two not quite so usual instruments. The singer was holding an accordion and stood next to him was a guy wearing a sheet of corrugated metal across his torso, playing it with what looked like a couple of spoons. This was a fast, rhythmic party music the likes of which I had never heard. Zydeco is the Creole music of New Orleans and Louisiana, and up in Memphis tonight was a Zydeco band called Dikki Du and the Zydeco Krewe. In front of the stage couples of all ages danced in armlock. All those weddings and parties I've been to with Mrs C where she has had to drag me up onto the dancefloor to stumble around self-consciously to music I don't like but which the majority of people consider to be party music. The tables were finally turned but she wasn't there. She still remembers receiving the unexpected text message I sent her in the early hours (UK time) from that bar in Memphis. 'I wish you were here; I want to dance with you.'

The following morning was an early start from Memphis AMTRAK station. Having picked up my tickets for AMTRAK's "City of New Orleans" train, depositing my case, I had time for a quick walk out. At least I could say I had seen the nearby Lorraine Motel, which was one of the hotels that catered for black Americans during the era of segregation. It was here that Dr Martin Luther King was assassinated and now in its place is the National Civil Rights Museum. A humbling place on an eerie, deserted winter's morning. Back at the station very soon I was "riding on the City of New Orleans" on the next leg of my adventure on the tracks of the Deep South.

Riding on the City of New Orleans

Good Morning America, How are you?
Don't you know me, I'm your native son,
I'm the train they call the City of New Orleans,
I'll be gone five hundred miles when the day is done.

Early morning Memphis. My bag has been checked in, but train 59 was delayed. The City of New Orleans train left Chicago yesterday afternoon and headed south through the night. AMTRAK services are often delayed though, but as long as you aren't in a hurry it's a great way to travel. The shiny silver giant finally arrived in Memphis and I made my way to my Coach Class seat. If you haven't ridden AMTRAK, the seats are in a pitch barely imaginable in Europe. Square-backed seats and roomy as heck, they recline seemingly close to horizontal, with foot and even leg rests to enable full long-distance relaxation.

No such horizontal reclining for me though. There was too much interest out of the window as we made our way through the state of Mississippi. It's a great journey through sleepy southern cotton fields and towns forgotten by the modern world, but it's also along a route that brought the Blues from humble backwaters to the world. Hazelhurst was the birthplace of Robert Johnson and McComb was home to Bo Diddley, according to the informative AMTRAK route guide. Eventually we cross into Louisiana and the highlight of the journey for me as we enter the bayou's other-worldly landscape of swamps and contorted cypress trees. The vegetation and the climate had changed dramatically by the time we made our final sweep hugging Lake Pontchartrain and into the Big Easy, the Crescent City, New Orleans.

My hotel was positioned with an entrance onto each of New Orleans' two most famous (or infamous) streets, Canal Street and Bourbon Street. I checked in, dropped off my bag, then headed out through the door into Bourbon Street. Into a kaleidoscopic corner of colour and craziness. The top end of Bourbon is a bit of an eye-opener and if I'm honest I felt a wee bit uncomfortable. This was the Big Easy in your face big time and with no filter. I walked briskly on, deciding that I'd have to find a different route for our genteel customers through the French Quarter and back onto Bourbon to miss out the racier bit outside our hotel door, which up to a point would remind European visitors of Amsterdam's Red Light District.

'Hey man, do you want some snow?'

A guy in a hooded top was now walking alongside me as I strode up Bourbon in the cold, wittering on about the weather. Now we Brits supposedly delight in talking about the weather, so I felt very much at home, telling him about the snowball fight I'd had the previous day in Memphis. Such unusual weather for the time of year in Tennessee. My new-found friend looked puzzled though.

'Do you want some snow, man, or not?'

My partner in precipitation-related conversation seemed to be getting a little agitated, almost as if he wasn't actually referring to the unseasonal weather further north, so I disappeared into the familiar, the soothing surroundings of a record shop.

My evening was spent on board the equally comfortable surroundings of a Mississippi paddle steamer, plying a tourist route along the river. Although the scenery isn't sparkling, it is an interesting trip. You always get a different perspective of a place from the water, plus this touristy experience involves dinner and jazz, an obvious choice for visitors and rightly so.

Back in my room on the corner of Canal and Bourbon I unpacked. American hotel rooms tend to be bigger than ours, often with two double or king-size beds. There is usually a very welcome coffee maker too, which is often missing in continental Europe. This particular room also came with a music system and CD player, a rare opportunity to try out the CD Keith had given me at the Country Music Hall of Fame back in Nashville a few days earlier, filled with the great and good of the genre. You live and learn from your mistakes. The nostalgic sentimentality of Country for family, loved ones, a simpler existence was not the right soundtrack for a dad missing his wife and daughters after a week of constant travel. It's these quiet pauses between all the frantic touring that hit you like a hammer. When everyone you need to help make things happen has finished their working day, returning home to their families and you are left stuck on your own in a hotel room with Dolly Parton.

Obviously, I don't mean the real Dolly Parton, though that particular scenario would have been the fantasy of many men of a certain age. I have nothing against Dolly either; you can't not admire the way she has used her fame to help other kids from the wrong side of the tracks. Her free book scheme 'The Imaginary Library' was tellingly launched in the UK in my hometown, Rotherham, and she is still well loved by even the most cynical of Yorkshire folk. No, Dolly wasn't there personally, but the sound system blasted out her sentimental epic. 'Coat of Many Colours', a tale of simple country life, poor folk making the best of things, a coat fashioned from bits of cloth by Dolly's sweet, beloved mother, brought the tears flooding again as I searched frantically for the remote control to turn the bloody thing off! I can almost hear my dad muttering, 'Pull yerself together, yer great soft lump!'

The following day was the start of the working week and my chance to visit a few potential hotels, the highlight of which was probably the

Hotel Monteleone in the heart of the French Quarter, but I admit mostly for its revolving circular bar that looks like a carousel. A crammed-in guided coach tour took me to the ornate tombs and mausoleums of New Orleans' cemeteries, also covering the devastation, human suffering and hardship left behind in Hurricane Katrina's wake. The Big Easy is a sobering mix of music lovers, thrill-seekers for whom every visit is mardi gras, but also of people trying to scrape a living any which way they possibly can.

After tucking into my new found Louisiana favourite, red beans and rice, at Café Maspero down on Decatur Street, I headed back along Canal Street for my final nightcap in NOLA. Coming towards me from the opposite direction was a big guy, well dressed, I presumed with his wife, also nicely attired, with broad, welcoming smiles on their faces.

'I bet you I can tell you where you got them shoes?' exclaimed my next French Quarter street conversationalist.

'Yeah right,' said I, knowing immediately I should have just walked on.

'Well, I'm a shoe-shiner by trade. If I give you the wrong answer I'll give you a free shoe-shine. If I'm right you'll pay for the shine.'

I don't think I even spoke, knowing I was being mugged. Whatever the answer would be, I had just fallen for a classic reserved only for the most naïve of tourists.

'You got that shoe owwwn that foot and the other shoe owwwn the other foot,' proclaimed the smiling assassin with delight.

A squirt of polish was applied to my Doc Martens and a rudimentary shine took place. I've rarely felt more uncomfortable than those few seconds on Canal Street. Not only was I being done over good and proper but, even more embarrassingly, picture a well-meaning white liberal European tourist stood in a public place with an African American guy crouched down, shining his shoes. Finally the ordeal was over. This was the gentlest of muggings, I suppose, and I was informed that the cost would be ten bucks. The hotel contracts negotiator in me (and skinflint Yorkshireman) automatically kicked in and the bill was reduced to $5. On reflection I should have just given the guy what he asked for. As I wrote earlier, the people of this city have been through times that are difficult for us to imagine. In the Big Easy there are those that need to hustle to survive.

The Crescent train departs New Orleans Union Station early morning bound for New York City, arriving the following day in the early afternoon. My journey would take me as far as Atlanta, back where this trip started, arriving in the early evening.

The big highlight of train 20's journey has to be the six mile crossing of Lake Pontchartrain, just after departure from New Orleans. A single track perched on a trestle surrounded by water, it's the longest railroad bridge in the United States and crosses the second largest saltwater lake in the country. It's a sociable experience travelling on AMTRAK and I enjoyed the company for a few stations of a guy who told me he was from Leeds. 'Me too,' said I, although we were of course referring to two different cities and, unfathomably, he had never heard of the original Leeds. Meridian, Tuscaloosa, Birmingham, we rolled across Alabama and back into Georgia. The sound of Georgian Otis Redding's Stax classic 'Sittin' on the Dock of a Bay' was ringing in my ears as we pulled into Atlanta, a fitting end to my 'Tracks of the Deep South'.

Chapter 9 - Love in the Lake District

Quick, close your eyes! Usher your children out of the room! This chapter starts with sex! Noisy sex. The noisiest sex ever.

It was nothing to do with me, of course. I was travelling alone (as usual). I'd just checked into my room in Carlisle at a hotel right next to the station. It's a nice enough abode and very well placed for a rail holiday. I ate there too and enjoyed the food. But my lasting memory is my first one. From down the corridor. I did go to check out where the hell it was coming from. Just in a professional capacity, you'll understand, to get a handle on how thick the walls were. There's no point putting your customers in rooms with paper thin walls where everyone can hear everyone else's private moments. But the walls here weren't paper thin. I wasn't holding glass against the door to eavesdrop, honest. There was no need to. She was screaming, he was grunting like a primate, the walls were rocking. Welcome to Border Country, an outpost of primal energy!

As we've begun this chapter with a bit of smut, it seems like a good time for a travel industry anecdote, a tale of legend that has done the rounds over the years, often being embellished but I heard it originally from the horse's mouth. Close colleagues in the industry will recognise the personality involved and they'll know I write this with affection for a friend, former colleague and mentor.

During my early years in travel I worked for a big, famous coach tour company in Leeds that sadly no longer exists. Its Hotel Contracts

Manager was a larger-than-life character. Multilingual, ruddy-faced, fiery, he was a man of some mystery. Continental in origin but when asked where he was from he would always sidestep the question with vagueness. It would seem that his roots lay somewhere along the Swiss-Belgian border. Make of that what you will. He never disclosed the truth. What was he hiding? Anyway, a keen cyclist (was he Belgian?), every year he would pack his bike into his company car and head to the port to drive around Europe for two or three months, hotel to hotel. He would return to Leeds eventually with a box full of signed hotel contracts and a boot filled with red wine to accompany his bike, no doubt gifted from hotels happy to see him and his contract.

So, 'Red Wine Rolf' (I've changed his name for anonymity purposes as he is sadly no longer with us) was staying in a Novotel somewhere, I forget where but it isn't important. As you'll know, most hotel rooms, particularly in corporate chains, adhere to a similar layout. There's a bed in the main part of the room and a little corridor with a bathroom to the left or right, and the external bedroom door straight ahead. Well, 'Red Wine Rolf', a man of a certain age and no doubt having imbibed a couple or six clarets, raised himself in the middle of the night for a tinkle. Business done, he walked the wrong way out of the loo. He took a left instead of a right. Out through the door. Out into the corridor. Into the public domain. As Rolf rubbed his eyes to see where he had landed in his morning stupor, the door closed behind him, destined not to open again without the help of a key card. But he had no key card. Nor a stitch of clothing to cover his, erm, man of a certain age! A man who had stayed at thousands of hotels in a career dating back to the 1960s found himself ruddy-faced, naked in the corridor of a hotel, walking to reception for a new key. A lifetime of contract wrangling, now just his accoutrements dangling. I can picture the receptionist asking, 'Can I help you, sir?'

Anyway, I digress. Again. The previous day I had explored the Cumbrian Coast Line, one of England's most remote and scenic branch lines. Staying in Kendal, I dropped my car in Millom and headed north on the Northern Rail service in the early morning bright sunshine glow of late spring. On such a fine day I admit that the Cumbrian Coast Line joined my top five UK rail experiences in no time. Imagine the glistening sea to the left and the fells of the Lake District to the right, as the train skirts the Irish Sea coast. At Ravenglass you can get off and join a little steam excursion into the fells on 'L'aal Ratty', the Ravenglass & Eskdale Railway. Then there's the curio of Sellafield, with workers hopping on and off pre and post-shift, the shock of human meddling interrupting the serene natural beauty of an otherwise untouched, unspoilt coast. At Whitehaven, still relatively early in the day, my stomach forced me off the train and into a greasy spoon café. Whitehaven and Workington are tough little towns, outposts nestled between inhospitable fells and the harsh sea.

Returning to Millom, I ended the day at the heritage Lakeside & Haverthwaite Steam Railway, which runs along a preserved former branch line of the Furness Railway to Lake Windermere, from where boats whisk you across the lake to Bowness on Windermere or onwards to Ambleside. At Haverthwaite they opened the sheds for me, with the unmistakable whiff of grease, oil and machinery, to have a look at the preservation taking place. I enjoyed tea and scones in their lovely station buffet before embarking on the steamy three-mile ride through the woodlands to Lakeside.

It is well worth the visit and an even better experience if you book a package with a boat trip too. You can also leave your car behind and have a great day out with one of the bundles organised by the railway, with added attractions along the way. At Lakeside you can visit the aquarium, whereas at the other side of the lake is the World of Beatrix Potter at Bowness for fans of all things twee. A mile's walk away from Haverthwaite station at the other end of the steam railway is the Lakeland Motor Museum with 30,000 exhibits of automotive memorabilia.

Whilst Bowness on Windermere doesn't have a rail connection, its neighbour up the hill, Windermere itself, sits at the end of the line bringing passengers to the Lake District from Kendal. Windermere is an attractive little town in its own right, but if you have just a short time, fancy some fresh air in your lungs and it's a clear day you can take a very easy, relatively short uphill walk to Orrest Head. I did just that, returning with my family last year in the glow of a crisp, clear

October day. The views from the top are a great introduction to the Lakes.

Back in Carlisle, it's a proud border city standing in a convenient spot for a rail holiday. The West Coast Mainline brings visitors from north and south, whereas it is also a start point of the Cumbrian Coast Line in one direction and the Hadrian's Wall Line heading eastwards across to Newcastle, another remote rail adventure to be ravished. They would call it bonny in those parts. And speaking of parts, whilst the duo down the corridor worked their parts I made do with ramparts at nearby Carlisle Castle. It's a fornication, sorry, I mean fortification dating from the 12th century and managed by English Heritage. So at least I got to improve my carnal knowledge, I mean my knowledge of Carlisle. Time to leave the border country, I think. Time to take a different ride.

Chapter 10 - I'm tired and I wanna go to Bled.

'**C**ome on Rob,' I hear you shortly cry, 'you're supposed to be telling us about all these amazing train journeys, filled with scenery to make your eyes pop out of their sockets, travelling at speed, with comfort and the added social aspect of sharing a long-distance rail experience with those in your near vicinity. So why are you banging on about your worst trip?!?'

Well, that's not strictly true. This wasn't my worst trip. It was a mind-blowing 24 hours, looking back, that much I can't deny. It did begin with a pretty grim experience on rails, but you tend to take the rough with the smooth when trying to position yourself somewhere for the next day at unsociable hours. Or indeed to check out a dicey journey that might not be suitable for paying customers as part of their holiday. There would be a few of these, the occasional bits of ridiculousness dotted amidst the undeniably vast expanses of rail-based sublime. So where do we begin?

Venice. Santa Lucia station, to be exact. It's the squat, concrete entry of choice for me to the city of canals and romance. This was the first time I had clapped eyes on the floating city and I have been back many times since. Venice has that kind of attraction. Now, I don't normally go for places filled with hordes of tourists and the cynical industry obsessed with extracting every spare penny from said tourists' pockets, but there is a reason why Venice is filled with tourists. It's just so damned special. Do you know what I love most about it? It's the simple pleasure of watching the boats come and go along the canals, going about their daily business. One of the few advantages of being poor at sleeping is that you get to be awake before the tourists to watch boats filled with cargo destined for hotels, restaurants and shops chugging up and down the canal; the secret freight boats preparing the city of romance for another day fulfilling the dreams of lovers yet to rise from their hotel beds.

I like Santa Lucia station. It's stark and modernist and has a strange appeal, given its surroundings. From its incongruous concrete forecourt you are led straight to the Grand Canal. Kaboom! There's Venice! Right there! In front of you! I had flown into Venice Marco Polo and, following a short transfer, was fortunate to have a couple of hours to wander amidst the alleys criss-crossing the famous canals before my direct evening train to Ljubljana. I was positioning myself to meet Milan from a Slovenian receptive tour operator the following morning at 7am sharp. My train would arrive in Ljubljana before midnight and the following day would be a long one, piecing together a new tour of the Balkans, inspired more than a little by Michael Palin's then recent 'New Europe' tv series.

The train on which I travelled no longer exists. I wonder whether this particular evening was the straw that broke the camel's back? Who knows? All I know is that I settled into my reserved seat and thought, "By jiminy, it's warm in here!" We waited. No movement. Sticking to our seats in the suffocating heat, Santa Lucia began dropping down my league table of favourite stations as we anticipated the departure of sauna on rails via Monfalcone, Gorizia (Gorica) and onwards to Ljubljana. With air-conditioning in our part of the train malfunctioning, carriages were closed due to Health & Safety and I found a seat on the floor of a vestibule for our three hour delayed departure, with no scenery to make my eyes pop out of my sockets, travelling at questionable speed, zero comfort and with the added social aspect of sharing a long distance rail experience with a frustrated mother and son combo arguing into the night.

Into the night indeed. It was 3am when we finally reached Ljubljana. My head hit the pillow on what would become my shortest ever overnight stay in a hotel. Immediately woken by an alarm, no time for breakfast, I went to find my travelling companion. Milan was waiting for me in reception, fresh as a daisy, a big welcoming smile on his face, the biggest smile in the Balkans, I'd say, and pumped up for the long day ahead. Jeepers.

What was Milan's first impression of me? Well, I'm not sure. A slightly dishevelled Brit with bloodshot eyes and general lethargy caused by the previous twelve hours on a vestibule floor? Milan was raring to get stuck into this new project and thankfully he had enough energy for both of us. We were about to piece together a unique new tour by rail (where possible) through the former Yugoslavia. The excitement of a new opportunity, the thrill of the chase for something fresh and different that I normally love.

Milan's car sped westwards, back towards regions through which 'that train journey' had brought me. Our first destination was Lake Bled, where we visited the stations in the countryside north of the lake that might be our customers' entry point, checking their suitability and accessibility, followed by five or six of the resort's hotels. Lake Bled really is Slovenia's jewel, with a perfect focal point in the middle of the lake, a wooded island topped by a medieval church. The glistening waters and general contented calm was enticing me to sneak off for a power nap, soothed by the lapping of water collected from the stunning surroundings of the Julian Alps. But no, I decided which hotel was most suitable for our groups and it was back into Milan's car, speeding eastwards whence we came. Time was in short supply that day.

It was lunchtime. Thank goodness. I hadn't eaten anything since Venice. Ljubljana, however brief the visit, was a joyful respite on that gorgeous summer's day. As a capital city it's manageable. In fact it has more of a feel of a provincial capital, which is, I suppose, exactly the role it played for many centuries. Its centre boasts baroque and art nouveau architecture and we ate in a relaxing setting overlooking the Ljubljanica river, which I found unusually serene for the middle of a capital city. And for those of us searching for rails wherever we venture, a funicular railway leads from the very centre of the city up to its crowning glory, the castle.

Two more hotels visited in Ljubljana in order to decide finally whether to base the groups in Bled or Ljubljana (I had pretty much already chosen the former, with a day excursion to Ljubljana), the crazy day continued. The irrepressible Milan dropped me off at Ljubljana station to meet my train to Zagreb. He wouldn't be travelling with me, instead belting down the motorway into Croatia to meet me at the other end, no doubt still jumping with enough energy for the two of us.

The EuroCity train had originated in Villach and was operating with Austrian rolling stock. For me there is somehow a soothing whiff of nostalgia on EuroCity services. They are the product of historic cross-border co-operation between national rail operators, requiring a certain level of speed, comfort and catering in order to carry the EC name. Equally appealing for me, the origins of the EuroCity system lie with the Trans Europ Express network, harking back to great days of European international rail travel, which were sadly over before my time. EuroCity trains are essentially cross-border Inter City services (rather than the high speed, ultramodern ICE or TGV trains). For those with a little more time to kill, EuroCity routes are a great way to explore Europe at a fast but not breakneck pace. An additional advantage for me is that, dependent on the operator or route, they occasionally use the nostalgic compartment-style carriages that I love.

The journey between these two now proud capitals of independent ex-Yugoslav states is a scenic one along the attractive Sava river valley and with a pre-alpine backdrop of rolling hills and meadows reminiscent in parts of Lower Austria. On the EuroCity it takes around 2 ½ hours. The stretch between Ljubljana and Zidani Most is particularly pretty, before approaching the Croatian border at Dobova and that other piece of nostalgic excitement, the arrival on the train of square-jawed, stern-faced Croatian border enforcers with scary guns, looking your embodiment of weariness up and down with disdain in an atmosphere crackling with tension, before stamping your passport, managing a knowing smirk and wishing you a pleasant stay. A little piece of theatre on rails.

Zagreb finally pulled into view and the train had beaten Milan's car to the Croatian capital, where my home for the night would be the Hotel Esplanade. Zagreb Glavni Kolodvor station is a grand building in its own right, but, situated opposite and at the head of the city's parkland on a grand tree-lined boulevard leading to the Old Town, the Esplanade is one of Zagreb's grandest art nouveau buildings. One of the great railway hotels, it was opened in 1925, having been built to service customers stepping off the Orient Express before those decades of political turmoil eventually confined that particular route to history. At check-in, still in need of that illusive second wind, I was offered a comfortable seat and a coffee whilst completing the paperwork. Now this is my kind of establishment. Coffee, I've since learned, is very much entwined with Croatian culture. After dining in the Esplanade's ornate restaurant I was very grateful to hit the very grand sack I had been afforded by the hotel at the end of a fascinating, full-on and fatiguing 24 hours.

The new day would bring a morning's work in Zagreb, before embarking on the next leg of the adventure, heading southwards to Split. These tracks lead right through a region that can bear witness to immense and relatively recent political turmoil and human suffering. With some trepidation, I admit, I had the feeling that the following 24 hours would be no less fascinating.

Chapter 11 - Split Personalities

The previous 24 hours had been testing to say the least, travelling overnight in a train vestibule from Venice to Ljubljana, viewing hotel after hotel in beautiful Bled and lovely Ljubljana, then hopping on another train to Zagreb for barely a night in what still remains my favourite hotel bar none, Zagreb's Hotel Esplanade. The next 24 hours would be thought-provoking beyond any other train journey I have ever made, with two very contrasting Croatian cities connected by a scenic line scarred physically and emotionally by relatively recent history.

A sunny Zagreb morning saw my Slovenian guide Milan drag me around another few hotels, all nondescript in comparison to the exquisite Esplanade in which we had stayed. It was a waste of a morning, to be fair, because I was already determined that the Esplanade was the one for our groups. Built for the Orient Express during the period when its route traversed Croatia, how could we stay anywhere else? Pleasant parks run down the middle of central Zagreb's wide main thoroughfares in grand central European fashion, harking back to the city's Habsburg past. Speaking of fashion, on walking past a tie shop Milan explained to me that 'cravat' was actually a word derived from 'Croat'. Apparently Croatian women had adorned their warrior males with a keepsake neckerchief before they rode off to war (probably against the Serbs). That's where it comes from. I've since googled it and it is true, a new fact for this particular fan of facts.

Back at Zagreb Glavni Kolodvor station I bade farewell to my Slovenian friend, Milan, who is indeed still a friend. I boarded the afternoon direct train to Split, a journey cutting due south from central Europe to the Mediterranean coast that would take all afternoon. The train was modern, commuter-style and German-built, reminiscent of the Transpennine Express trains back in the UK which would take me from Leeds to places like York or Manchester for work or days out. It was reasonably comfortable and air-conditioned, which was a godsend in the oppressive heat of this July day. It is a long journey, the train never reaching a speed you might expect from a long-distance ride between a country's two main conurbations, but it's certainly a scenic one, trundling through backwaters of rural Croatia not too distant from the Bosnian border.

This is the former Yugoslavia though, scene of unimaginable acts of cruelty in a war not long ago, and along the route are buildings left to ruin, ominous signs of the region's tragic recent past. It seems crass to offer a potted history of the Balkan countries, but there may be people reading this who weren't around in the early 1990s or aren't generally aware of the history of the region, so I will try to do it with respect and impartiality.

I hate the term 'ethnic cleansing'. It was used in the media non-stop during and after the Balkan conflicts, mainly aimed at Serb nationalists who, after the fall of the Soviet Bloc and the breakdown of Yugoslavia, sought to reclaim territories either bound within their own historical ideal of nationhood or in which there existed ethnic Serb communities. 'Ethnic cleansing' is a term used to describe the dispersal of a neighbouring people from their homes, or, worse still, the bloodshed or torture and even genocide inflicted on that people by their neighbour. To gain support for and to validate their actions, criminals need to dehumanise their victims. By using terms like 'ethnic cleansing' we are contributing to this cycle of dehumanisation. Expulsion, torture, rape, murder, genocide are better words, however unpalatable, for the acts perpetrated on neighbours between 1991 and 1995.

In our safe western European homes we saw night after night the unspeakable scenes from a war taking place on our own continent, yet distant and unfathomable. Weren't the Serbs and Croats neighbours?

Didn't they speak a very similar language? What was it about? Here goes. The Croats are predominantly Catholic and have generally looked culturally towards central Europe; the Serbs are predominantly Orthodox and look towards Mother Russia. During the First World War the Croats fought alongside the Austro-Hungarian troops in the Axis, whereas the Serbs joined the Allied forces. After all, the war was sparked by a Serb nationalist assassinating Austro-Hungarian Archduke Franz Ferdinand in Sarajevo. During World War Two in annexed Croatia the country was split between the Nazi and Fascist regimes and a horrible Nazi puppet government called Ustaše ruled, victimising the usual Nazi victims, plus Serbs. In Serbia the nationalist Chetnik movement grew strong, offering resistance, but also collaborating with the Nazis when it suited them. The Chetnik of Serb folklore was a warrior fighting for a Greater Serbia, and Croats and Bosnians were their own victims of choice. In the aftermath of the war Marshall Tito, an ethnic Croat, managed to keep the peace within a Soviet Bloc Yugoslavia where the past was brushed under the carpet. When Yugoslavia disintegrated all hell broke loose. And what a hell.

The Serb war crimes are well-documented. Srebrenice, Vukovar, many more. Mass killings to a scale beyond all comprehension. But the train line between Zagreb and Split crosses through a region of 'ethnic cleansing' less well known in the West. The region is called 'Krajina' by the Serbs, literally 'border area'. There were many ethnic Serb communities there and in 1990 the region was seized by ethnic Serb separatists, dispersing their Croat neighbours from their homes and with the bloodshed and murder of Croat civilians. The Croat forces responded with 'Operation Storm', a blitzkrieg which drove Serbs from this land and which resulted in the massacre of Serb civilians in and around Karlovac, Gospić and Knin, all of which sit on this otherwise unassuming, scenic rural railway line. 'Operation Storm' resulted in up to 200,000 Serb civilians leaving Croatia.

Early evening Split station in the Mediterranean heat of July. After a thought-provoking journey, to say the least, this British travel professional lugged his case off the train, trussed up in shirt (though no cravat), trousers and linen jacket, the latter being the only nod to the temperatures in which we would be working. My guide for Split, Ivica, stood grinning on the platform in shorts and tee-shirt, sweat patches under his armpits.

'What the hell are you wearing, man?! Are you crazy?! It's July!'

He had a point. I was the archetypal stuffy Englishman, totally not dressed for the local climate. I may as well have been wearing a bowler hat and three-piece suit.

I learned a lot from Ivica over the next 36 whirlwind hours in Split. We had so much in common. We were a similar age and we both loved football. Ivica was a big fan of local heroes, Hajduk Split, a club with an interesting history and to be a supporter of Hajduk would have been at certain points in time a massive two fingers to whichever regime was ruling.

Hajduk was formed by a group of students from Split in exile in the famous U Fleků brewery tavern in Prague. By the way, if you are ever in Prague make sure you visit U Fleků for that authentic Czech tavern experience, with hearty (if a bit stodgy) food and the best dark Czech beer to wash it down.

Anyway, I digress. Again. Back in the 1940s the Axis powers annexed Croatia and Split was to be governed by the Italian fascist Mussolini. Hajduk Split was offered a place in the Italian Serie A football league on the proviso that they would change their name to AC Spalato (the Italian name for Split). Hajduk refused. The Italian dictator responded by forming his own club in Split and moving into Hajduk's stadium, even naming the stadium after his sons. The people of Split had lost their home, their independence and even their football club.

Unable to meet in Split itself due to the war, Hajduk players came together on the island of Vis, together with Tito, leader of the Partisan resistance, and British officers including the son of Winston Churchill. That night it was announced that Hajduk Split would reform and become the team of the Yugoslav resistance against fascism.

It is also said that after the war Tito offered his favoured club the opportunity to move to the new Yugoslav capital, Belgrade in Serbia, to become the team of the people's army. As you might expect from the Hajduk Split story so far, they stuck to their guns, remained in Split, and the army club Partizan Belgrade was formed instead.

Hajduk became very successful in the 1970s, winning four Yugoslav league titles and five cups, also reaching the latter stages of the European competitions. Recent years have been turbulent though, with a rapid decline in sporting standards, plus a string of financial problems that have threatened to ruin the club.

The Hajduk fans are an interesting bunch too to say the least. In the 1950s, inspired by Brazilian fans creating a carnival atmosphere at the 1950 World Cup, the fan group Torcida was formed to replicate South American style fandom on the Dalmatian coast. Since then, though, Croatian football has been plagued by problems such as hooliganism, violence and the rise of the far-right. Hajduk fans and Torcida are far from immune from these social problems. Looking around Split back then, around 2009, I saw quite a few tee-shirts bearing the name "Hajduk Jugend", a miserable reflection on how it seemed acceptable in Croatia to use inflammatory Nazi language and imagery.

Back to Ivica, as well as football we had music in common too. He was a big fan of the British post-punk scene and the seminal Manchester band Joy Division in particular. In most Soviet-era Eastern Bloc countries western music had been difficult to access, but Ivica told me that Tito's regime had been much more relaxed than those of Yugoslavia's neighbours.

But that's where the similarities in our lives ended. It became clear that Ivica and I had experienced very different lives through our early 20s. Whilst I had been living the life of Reilly at Leeds University, state-subsidised by a student grant, attending lectures when I could be bothered and cutting gangly nocturnal shapes on dancefloors in dark basement clubs in my safe western European home, Ivica had been fighting a bitter war that clearly still left deep scars, particularly when he described the Serb shelling of Dubrovik, the Croatian jewel of the Dalmatian coast.

What a city is Split though! Imagine a busy Dalmatian port, nearby beaches and resorts, a big city sprawled behind heading inland, but facing the sea the incredible Diocletian Palace. Covering a huge part of Split's Old Town, it's a Roman city fortress really, built in the 4th century for the Emperor Diocletian. When Split became part of the Venetian sphere of influence the Venetians built their own city within the stunning ancient Roman walls. I was gobsmacked by this place. I had expected to be blown away by the next ancient city on my itinerary, Dubrovnik, but Split's Old Town was every bit as beautiful and, for me anyway, more interesting.

The hotel visits were a tad more relaxed. I may have even loosened my tie. Mediterranean-style, we took a mid-day break, heading up into the hills overlooking Split to a grill restaurant, once again hammering home the huge cultural differences of Croatia. The food of the south is the food of the Mediterranean, with grilled fish and meat dominating menus, plus Croatian wine as accompaniment. Zagreb had been much more central European, harking back to an Austro-Hungarian past. Like France or Italy in many ways, Croatia has a deep-rooted north-south divide of a serious stoic or industrious north and carefree Mediterranean south.

The hotel that sticks out most in my memory was the last one we visited. Brand new, only just opened, the air conditioning was a huge respite on a blistering hot July day. It had in total 99 rooms, plus two suites.

'That makes 101 Dalmatians!' said the hotelier.

Next stop Dubrovnik, the jewel in Croatia's Dalmatian coast crown and at the time of my trips an arduous car journey along an undeveloped coast road. Since then the road has been massively upgraded and journey times reduced. It was, and still is, possible to take a ferry from Split to Dubrovnik, sailing along the coast and amidst idyllic islands increasingly popular in their own right with tourists. I had already decided that that's exactly what our customers would do to reach the climax of their yugotour, but in the absence of a railway linking the two Dalmatian cities I elected to return home for the weekend, revisiting Dubrovnik whistle-stop a couple of weeks later.

Which is exactly what I did. No hold luggage. No hand luggage apart from my work bag. A toothbrush, a bedshirt and a change of socks and underwear were packed into my satchel and I flew late evening into Dubrovnik for a 24-hour recce.

Staying on the Arpad peninsula out of town I managed an early morning walk along the coast, checking out the curious concrete ledges perched at the bottom of the cliffs, the local version of a beach.

Fortified by breakfast at my hotel that included the even more curious option of cold broccoli on the buffet (last night's leftovers?), I managed to visit around ten hotels and take a little siesta admiring Dubrovnik's Old Town, restored to its former glory after the bombardment of Serb shells during the Balkan Conflict.

Dubrovnik was impressive and I had no doubt it would be the mighty climax to the tour for many of our customers, but sometimes it's the surprise packages that live longer in the memory. Split had been one of those surprise packages and Dubrovnik, for all its undoubted honeypot beauty, was a return to mass tourism after Bled, Zagreb and Split on what had been extraordinary and thought-provoking journey through the former Yugoslav states.

Chapter 12 - Caledonia Dreaming Part 3 - London to Thurso and beyond

L et me introduce John. He's a likeable chap from a garage in Brora, a small town on the Sutherland coast north of Inverness and the only place locally from where you can hire a car. In this scene he is trying to reassure me. I'm arranging to hire a Ford Ka from him by phone. It's the only car available for hire in Brora. Concerned that I would possibly be arriving back late into Brora to drop off the car at the end of the day's hire and after his garage closure time, unable to hand deliver the keys to him, his nonchalant response?

"Just leave the car unlocked in the station car park with the keys under the visor. I'll pick it up the next day."

"Ohhhh Kayyyy! So I leave the car unlocked with the keys inside overnight in a public car park! Erm, right, so can I pay you by credit card now over the phone?"

"Sorry, we don't have that facility. Nae problem though. Just leave the £50 with the keys in the car in the station car park," replied laidback John.

"Are you sure? So I leave the car unlocked in a public place, with the keys and £50 under the visor?!"

"Dinnae worry, son. There is no crime in Sutherland!"

It is another world.

This trip started in London with the Caledonian Sleeper, one of only two sleeper services still in existence in Britain. The new owner of the franchise has recently upgraded with brand new and very impressive looking units, which I'll describe once I've ridden them. But this journey was on the old-style sleeper and, as it was my first journey on a UK sleeper train, I detoured down to London to get the whole experience (you can also catch it in the north, more of which in another chapter).

Departing London Euston just after 9pm, you are shown to your cabin. There is a lower berth and a pull-down upper berth, storage space and a sink that converts to a table by the picture window. Showers and toilets are along the carriage and the bar car is a great way to meet fellow travellers and share stories. In those days Caledonian Sleeper compartments were all the same, with Standard Class accommodating two people and First Class the same cabin but for just one person. The train stops at Crewe and Preston, before splitting in the wee small hours in the Central Belt, one section heading along the West Highland Line at breakfast-time to Fort William, another section along the North Sea coast to Aberdeen, and mine would allow me views of the Cairngorms in the early morn en route to Inverness.

I won't deny it. The uncoupling and coupling in the middle of the night did disturb my Caledonian dreams, but I soon rolled back off, waking again in the brilliant sunshine and dewdrop dawn of the Grampians. Leisurely enjoying breakfast by my window, I admired old friends, Dalwhinnie and Aviemore before we rolled into Inverness.

After a morning revisiting Inverness hotels I boarded the ScotRail "Far North Line" service. The train would terminate in Thurso in distant Caithness, but my own journey would halt for the night in Brora. Leaving Inverness the Far North Line follows the Beauly Firth to Beauly itself, a station so tiny that the diddy platform cannot accommodate groups. At Dingwall, a junction town, the Kyle Line heads west across the mountains to the sea at Kyle of Lochalsh, but that's another story. From Dingwall the Far North Line veers back to the coast, skirting the Cromarty Firth, where the natural beauty of its watery landscape is sometimes obscured by the incongruous industrial sight of redundant oil rigs moored temporarily off-shore. For the next part of the journey you are never far from water, from the Dornoch Firth to the Kyle of Sutherland to the North Sea itself. The railway takes a different route to the A9 on many parts of this journey and is infinitely more scenic.

Dunrobin is worth a stop if you have time. It's a halt rather than a scheduled stop and it's only possible to alight there in the summer tourist season. Dunrobin is the seat of the Duke of Sutherland. The station was originally built as the Duke's private station and from here it is a just short walk across the road, through the grand entrance to the remarkable French-style château. The station itself is a listed building, whose Arts & Crafts style waiting room dates from 1902. My day ended at Brora though, a sleepy coastal town, where I'd meet chilled-out John the following morning, pick up the only car available for hire in Sutherland, then leave it unlocked, with the keys and £50 cash inside at the end of the day.

The following day was simple but hectic. Pick up the Ford Ka, drive up to visit hotels in Wick and Thurso, pop into the Castle of Mey, then back to Brora in time for the last train south. I'll admit that I detoured for a sneaky peek at John O'Groats too, but I've been back since to spend a bit more quality time in Caithness, such is its remote allure.

Whilst the road to the far north follows the coast into Caithness the Far North Line takes an altogether different route through a region known as the Highland Flow, a vast area of peat boglands virtually uninhabited by humans but a remarkable and important habitat for birdlife. From Georgemas Junction the train heads either to Wick or Thurso, the UK mainland's northernmost station and gateway to the Northern Isles from the nearby port of Scrabster. The Far North Line could definitely be described as a journey, from the city of the Highlands past Sutherland's coastal treats, then across bleak boglands to the edge of this island. But why stop there?

Northlink operates ferry services that are a lifeline to locals living in the Orkneys and Shetlands, but which provide us grateful tourists with a chance to sample an even more remote corner of the British Isles. Leaving Scrabster, make sure you are on the starboard side of the ship for close-up views of the Old Man of Hoy, one of the tallest sea stacks in Britain at 450 feet. The Orkneys themselves offer miles and miles of untouched beauty, with a stunning drive along the Churchill Barriers, constructed during the WWII to protect the port at Scapa Flow, the incredible Italian Chapel, built in the same period by homesick Italian prisoners of war, and the mystery of neolothic sites and stone circles scattered around the peaceful green islands.

But Orkney was a subsequent trip. This one ended back in Brora in the early evening. The only mystery to me is whether the car, the keys and the £50 cash were still in the station car park the following day. I never heard back from John, so can only assume everything was still there. It truly is another world.

Chapter 13 - Caledonia Dreaming Part 4

I t had seemed like a good idea when I booked it. I'd done the Caledonian Sleeper before from London, so this time I thought I would just meander across to Preston on a Northern Rail service over the Pennines on a Sunday evening, catching the Caledonian Sleeper at its last English joining point just after midnight.

It was a balmy summer's evening. Hours were whiled away in a pub close to Preston station watching Spain hammer Italy in the European Championship final. Still hours left before my train would arrive and the finally the wrong side of a locked pub door, I stumbled upon a curious sculpture outside the Preston Corn Exchange that caused a stir in me. It is an alarming scene of unarmed men, terror etched into their faces, prostrate in front of the guns of the establishment.

In 1842 Preston cotton mill workers went on strike in protest at huge wage cuts. The resulting stand-off and civil unrest resulted in the mayor ordering the military to fire on the protestors. In a scene reminiscent of the Peterloo Massacre, John Mercer, William Lancaster, George Sowerbutts and Bernard McNamara, the youngest at 17 years of age, were killed. The Preston Martyrs Memorial now stands on Lune Street outside the Corn Exchange, where the men were shot. It is a rare reminder of how the freedom and rights we now take for granted were won at great cost by our ancestors. People's history and the battle for suffrage in this country, which in turn shaped our society, are generally ignored by our history books and so monuments such as the Lune Street

Memorial deserve to be cherished. Clearly, I choose unusual places to hang out on late Sunday evenings after pub closing, but I am glad I did.

The Sleeper finally arrived in Preston, I boarded and, despite the clattering in the early morning as the train was split, before I knew it I was in Pitlochry. I picked up a car and headed west. After a night in Oban, the hotel for the second night would be near Duror between Oban and Fort William, whose very keen new owner had been badgering me for business. The drive westwards along Loch Tay from Kenmore to Killin was jaw-droppingly gorgeous. Next stop Crianlarich, then Tyndrum, Dalmally and finally Oban, with varying success hotel-wise. The next day, as mum looms large whenever I am north of the border, I managed a little time for thought at Connel Beach, where we had scattered her ashes amongst the pebbles a few years earlier in a place she loved. My meandering route then headed to Duror for my strangest night in a hotel and one that still haunts me to this day.

It was in the middle of nowhere, on the road between Oban and Fort William, as previously mentioned, but with nothing else of note around it. The drive led up to the hotel through pleasant gardens. All good so far. Parking up, I noticed peacocks loose in the grounds. A little unusual, but endearingly so. I pushed the door into Reception. And pushed. And pushed. The brand new carpet clearly hadn't been fitted to allow the main door customers would use to enter the hotel to pass over it. I put my shoulder to work and got through, centimetre by centimetre. A little unusual, I thought, though not quite so endearing. My room had a door that had been stripped to the grain, then painted over haphazardly with a thin layer of brown paint. Brown, I tell you. Was this shabby chic? The sign on the bedroom door was one of those plastic oblongs you would have seen on my childhood bedroom door back in the 1970s with "Robert" written on it and maybe a picture of a car. Whilst my name wasn't on this one, just a number, I recall there was a picture of a car! Was this retro? The room itself was....well, I just mentioned shabby chic....it was one of those words but not the other.

This was the only time in a hotel when I've considered escape. Escape from the middle of nowhere, escape from my childhood bedroom but without the comforting Rotherham United poster, escape from the peacocks and the hotel door that required the assistance of the Scotland rugby forwards to break into reception. But I didn't leave. Where else would I go? Travelling alone can occasionally, only occasionally, feel like a lonely existence. I missed mum. I missed my wife and I missed my daughters. I like my own company, but for once this isolation was anything but splendid. I braced myself and headed for the dining room.

The dining room was rammed with a German coach party. The staff consisted of a small group of Bangladeshi guys, totally rushed off their feet, but incredibly polite and willing to please. The food was a hearty version of meat and two veg. The desert was buffet style and one of the choices was a little pot of yoghurt from Aldi with the price tag still on it. 13p. Crikey, I felt special.

I retired to my childhood bedroom ready for the following day's meeting with the hotelier, a businessman new to the hotel trade, having already formed my opinion that I would nod politely, spout some platitudes, then run for the hills at the first opportunity.

A wake-up call wasn't necessary. At 4am there was a peacock screeching outside my window, the bright sunshine of midsummer in Scotland streaming through the wafer-thin curtains of my childhood bedroom. Breakfast was hearty full-Scottish, served by the same extremely polite, willing and hard-working Bangladeshi lads who had checked me in, served me dinner, tended the bar until late, etc.

The hotelier arrived and beckoned me into his office. A charming man, he told me that he only employed people from back home in Bangladesh because the locals were, in his words, lazy. He was quite desperate for business, so I nodded, spouted platitudes, then made haste back down the drive as soon as I could, dodging the peacocks, heading back to civilisation.

Something wasn't quite right there and I wasn't going to hang around to find out what it was. The reality is sobering. The hotelier was jailed in 2015 for three years on the charge of human trafficking. The reports I have read describe how he had exploited four men, charging them a huge amount of money to travel to Britain for work, paying them lower salaries than expected and making them work excessive hours. The tale of the Bangladeshi lads I had met is now a harrowing one;

expecting a new life and a job in a hotel in a British city, they were stuck miles away from anywhere, unable to speak to anyone about their plight, working sometimes eighteen hours a day, sleeping on hotel room floors, gardening, cooking, cleaning, waiting. Four guys with hopes and dreams of a better life. It was ironic that this trip had begun with Chartist rebellions in Preston against the exploitation of workers, yet it later transpired that I had witnessed first-hand what the press has since reported as 'modern day slavery'. I had driven away from Duror in relief that I would never have to go back again to the worst hotel in which I had ever stayed. Hindsight has revealed that it was far worse than I could ever have imagined.

Next stop Fort William, then the wonderful drive parallel to the West Highland Line through Glenfinnan to Mallaig, detouring around Loch Morar, Scotland's fifth largest loch and the deepest freshwater body in the British Isles. On this sunny July afternoon there wasn't a ripple to be seen; it was a picture of serenity, perfect peace, splendid isolation. Holed up in nearby Mallaig for the night in a less challenging hotel, I dined whilst gazing out to the following day's adventure, Skye.

Mallaig is the end of the line for the West Highland Railway northern branch. It's a place to arrive hungry, as the fish and chips are legendary. Whilst the fishing boats still search for their catch, Caledonian MacBrayne operates a couple of services out of Mallaig's ferry harbour. The Small Isles of Rhum, Eigg and Muck can be reached for those with time to spare. But as my day would end in Beauly I had to make do with the short crossing to Armadale on the southern tip of Skye. Driving across the island to the Skye Bridge, I rejoined the mainland, then chugged across the mountains, occasionally criss-crossing the Kyle Line, that other great railway journey of Scotland.

The Kyle Line is a true coast-to-coast experience. Leaving behind the magnificent views of Skye from Kyle of Lochalsh, you are quickly met with another highlight, the picturebook village of Plockton, set in a sheltered bay, complete with palm trees. If it seems familiar, the tv series Hamish Macbeth and the film The Wicker Man were filmed here. From Plockton Loch Carron dominates the next leg of the journey on the left side as the train heads for the wild mountains and forests, with views of the great Torridon Peaks in the distance. Next up is Loch

Luichart before we reach Dingwall, with mighty Ben Wyvis in the distance to the north. The train then glides along the southern shore of the Beauly Firth to approach Inverness, some 80 miles from its starting point.

But my day ended in Beauly with a visit to its two hotels and the ruined priory. It is said that Mary Queen of Scots dubbed it "beau lieu" (beautiful place) during a visit. Whilst it is a pleasant enough town, and I would stay there again, it is not ideal for rail groups as the station platform isn't big enough. I was there searching for an alternative to Inverness, but every day of the itinerary would have begun and ended with pointless coach transfers to and from Inverness anyway. That said, I enjoyed my stay at the coaching inn owned by the Frasers of Lovat and serving produce grown and reared on their estate. This being Thursday and high summer, the added spectacle of the Beauly Pipers marching down the High Street to the Main Square was a real bonus. There is something about pipe bands that stirs me and I can feel the goosebumps as I write this.

The A9 took me back through the Grampians, roughly following the railway track. Aviemore, Dalwhinnie, Kingussie and down to Pitlochry. I took in Queen's View on the outskirts of Pitlochry, the fantastic vista across the lochs to distant Rannoch. Up in the hills above Pitlochry is the Edradour Distillery, at that time, before the resurgence of small artisan distillers, the self-styled 'smallest distillery' in Scotland, with a crisp single malt hand-made by three men in the peaceful pretty haven. Not for the first time my tour ended without a dram, just a pleasant but annoyingly soft drink before I got back behind the wheel, back down to town. Base for the final night was the Atholl Palace, one of those wonderful Victorian era Scottish hydropathic spa hotels, a grand baronial style building so steeped in history that it has its own museum in the former staff quarters in the basement.

I have been back many times and will continue to do so. Four chapters into my Caledonian dream and I haven't even mentioned the coastal views from the train heading over the Tay Bridge and onwards past links courses to Aberdeen. Or the golden October of autumn colours in the Galloway Forest, just off the Burns Country Line. Or Ardnamurchan Point, the wild western tip of Scotland. Or the stunning

Isle of Mull, where the charming chieftain of the Clan MacLean, Lachy, showed us around his home, Duart Castle. I think there are many more Caledonian adventures still to come.

Chapter 14 - Norway by Boat, Bus & Train

A s a kid in the Deep South (of Yorkshire) I had a couple of obsessions. Football was the first, although I wasn't particularly good at it. Dad had been a goalkeeper in the local leagues. His favourite football yarn was of having trials with Wolverhampton Wanderers in his teens. Wolves had scouts in the mining villages, exploiting the natural seams of raw talent, tough lads from tough towns that needed a bit of process and polish before fuelling the fires of professional football clubs. Dad would only tell half the tale though, ending in flippant fashion that he met mum, decided to abandon Wolves and stay local, standing between the sticks at Thurcroft Miners Welfare. The truth is that the Wolves youth coach dad encountered was a tyrant, that dad tired quickly of his rants and mental cruelty, staying put much to the distaste of grandad, who then forbade him to play football, having thrown away a great opportunity. Dad would sneak out anyway, hiding his kit up his jumper, cleverly avoiding the local side, secretly keeping goal for the next village instead.

I was earmarked by my school team's manager to follow his footsteps into the goal. Goalkeepers were hard to find, but I had my own plans, a cultured left foot and dreamed of playing on the left wing. Alas, a lack of pace and physical strength left me on the sidelines, but it didn't matter as football was everywhere back then. There was a path running past the local playing fields. You would walk down and just join in. Mid-afternoon on Sundays the blokes would roll past on their way home from a lunchtime session at the Working Men's Club, taking off their jackets and simply wading in, five pints of Stones Best Bitter sloshing around in their bellies as they slid into a tackle. Ouch. It could end up twenty-a-side with an age range between ten and fifty and, yes, it was jumpers for goalposts!

My other obsession as a ten-year-old was the flimsy orange atlas that I devoured every evening after school, memorising the capital cities of countries I assumed I had no chance of ever visiting. The flimsy orange thing was usurped one Christmas by a big, bulky atlas inscribed, 'To Robert for Christmas '81, from Aunty Monica & Uncle Phillip'. I still have it.

Penfriends followed, often from quite exotic places. Well, anywhere is exotic when you are from Rotherham. There was Petri from Kuusamo in Finland. His first letter told me that his father was a 'saw working man' and his mother a 'charlady'. Kuusamo was irritatingly just off the edge of the Finland page of Aunty Monica and Uncle Phillip's big swanky atlas, close to the border of the Soviet Union, but I imagined a simple life in snowbound forests of the frozen north under the watchful gaze of the Kremlin.

There was also some kid in Kansas City who only wrote once in wonky, swirly, wibbly-wobbly lines. There was Benoit from Strasbourg too and Roland from Mannheim in Germany, but the longest correspondence was with Anna from Gothenburg, a rather beautiful Swedish girl with what sounded like a very rich dad. My letters to Anna fizzled out when I went to university, but it is no coincidence that my two most memorable penpals were from the mysterious northern climes of Scandinavia.

Norway was also a mystery to me as a child. Blue Peter would inform us every year that the Christmas tree in Trafalgar Square was a gift from the people of Norway. Oh, and a very ordinary England football team was beaten by Norway's underdogs, prompting a beautiful and infamous rant from the Norwegian commentator, Bjørge Lillelien, telling Lady Diana and Maggie Thatchoooor that their 'boys took one hell of a beating'! Bjørge was clearly a man on a mission.

Arriving at Oslo Airport the locals returning to Norway on my flight were also clearly on a mission, frantically emptying the Duty Free shop between airside and Arrivals, filling their baskets with alcohol with an intensity of purpose. A bit of a cultural curio, I thought, and passed through Arrivals into the Oslo evening, keen to get to my hotel, none other than the Grand Hotel on Karl Johansgate, the city's main drag.

I had many hotel visits the next day, though none more interesting than my host hotel. It is as grand as its name suggests, dating from the 1870s and the kind of place where you can imagine sitting with a coffee at the table next to Henrik Ibsen or a new Nobel Prize laureate or a foreign dignitary. And speaking of the Nobel Prizes, I was shown the Nobel Suite itself, where the prizewinners stay, and stood on the balcony overlooking the parliament building and Karl Johansgate below. It's from this balcony that the winners receive their ovations. For a few moments my mind slipped into dreamland and the hotel's Sales Manager's patter faded into the distance. There I was picking up the Nobel Price for Hotel Contracting, waving to my adoring followers in the street below. As I cleared my throat to make my speech reality returned. "A-hem!" The Sales Manager cleared his throat too and dragged me back inside, back into the reality of a day looking around identikit rooms at identikit corporate hotels.

I did manage a break to walk out to the Vigeland Sculpture Park, where 200 bronze, granite and cast iron sculptures created by Gustav Vigeland are installed within Frogner Park. Did I mention that the statues are naked? It's an expression of the human form and some of the sculptures are pretty surreal, not least on a crisp Scandinavian winter's day. I did consider lending 'Angry Boy' my coat. No wonder he was cross, being made to stand in the altogether in the freezing cold. Poor lad.

The next day promised an epic journey. I joined the Dovrebanen Railway at Oslo Sentral station after breakfast. NSB, the Norwegian State Railway (just rebranded 'Vy') provides comfortable accommodation on its long-distance trains, many of which cut through incredible scenery to match the great Swiss journeys. Standard Class is perfectly fine and, although there is a small First Class section, the difference was a leather seat, a coffee and a newspaper in a language I don't understand, so I was happy where I was in Standard.

Leaving Oslo the train glides along the sleepy waters of the Mjøser lake, bound for Hamar, which some of you may be interested to know is the home of the Norwegian Railway Museum. Next stop conjures up winter adventure – Lillehammer – before we head through the wilderness of Norwegian national parks to Otta and beyond to Dombås in the shadow of the Dovre National Park, arriving some four hours later. The Dovrebanen would then continue to Trondheim, the terminus of its Herculean seven hour journey, but I jumped off in Dombås to check out a very scenic branch line instead, the Raumabanen Railway.

The modern commuter-style trains of the Raumabanen ply the route from Dombås to Åndalsnes, just shy of 1 ½ hours of remote and rocky landscapes. It's 71 miles of contrasts, with jagged mountains reflected in the calm and clear waters of the Rauma River, wild national parks stretching into the distance, and well worth the detour.

It wasn't strictly a detour for me though on this sunny late winter's day. From Åndalsnes, my research told me, there would be a service bus that would shuttle me to my next destination, Ålesund. Or so I hoped. There wasn't much in Åndalsnes and, with a packed day ahead tomorrow in Ålesund I could really do with this bus existing. After initial doubt it arrived and whisked me away along Romsdalsfjorden to a jewel of a town I was looking forward to visiting.

There had been snowfall, so with darkness falling as my bus approached Ålesund, the city sat resplendent in its winter coat. We passed the football stadium and the floodlights were burning bright. "Great! Maybe there's a game on that I can see this evening!" I thought, before the realisation hit that the Norwegian leagues are played in the summer months for obvious reasons. Duh.

I wandered out to get something to eat. Pizza, just a Margherita at that, for £25. Gulp. That's dough with some cheese, tomatoes and herbs. £25. Imagine how this Yorkshireman's jaw dropped when he saw that! The next day brought a thaw and resultantly a very wet trudge around hotels, one of which had a pretty special annexe, the room in the lighthouse at the end of the quay! I did manage a squelchy wet climb up the 418 steps to Aksla Viewpoint, from where you can get a great perspective of the town, its archipelago and the surrounding Sunnmøre Alps. The main attraction of Ålesund itself is an attractive array of Art

Nouveau buildings, huddled around a pretty backdrop of maritime life in a climate ranging from harsh to sublime.

The next adventure began late at night. I had booked a night on the Hurtigruten coastal ship, which was scheduled to arrive at Ålesund at half past midnight. If you don't know Hurtigruten, it's a great way to see Norway's coast and fjords. It's actually a fleet with a number of vessels of varying sizes, providing a dual service. Its raison d'être is to provide a lifeline for coastal communities, delivering the goods (dough, cheese, tomatoes, herbs?) that keep them in existence, whilst simultaneously offering travellers an amazing coastal adventure from Norway's second city, Bergen, right up to North Cape and Kirkenes in a land far beyond the Arctic Circle, stopping at many points in between.

Having checked out of my hotel around 14 hours earlier, filling the day visiting other hotels, the last few hours of kicking around in anticipation of the next leg had dragged. Standing on an eerie quayside in the cold at gone midnight, wondering whether this now late ship would arrive, anticipation turned to anxiety. But the Hurtigruten ship did eventually roll in, I boarded my night boat and checked into my cabin, which was a comfortable if not plush outside cabin with two lower berths and a window. If you are expecting cruise ship style accommodation, then this isn't for you. There's no faded celebrity crooning in a distant bar, no attempt at the mass market, just a good standard of accommodation, meals and lounges, and the genuine experience of extraordinary coastline outside your window.

I wouldn't rush to eat whale meat again. Apologies to the vegetarians reading this. Whilst not vegetarian, I don't eat much meat myself, but it was there and I was intrigued, much as I had been with reindeer as the staple food further north. Please don't tell my kids I ate Rudolph, by the way! Anyway, back to whale….this delicacy had the texture of rubber. Well, while the whale digested I whiled away a morning watching the Norwegian coast gently pass by, arriving in Bergen in mid-afternoon.

Late afternoon I witnessed the setting sun across the quays from the top of Mount Fløyen, reached by funicular railway from a base station in the heart of Bergen's UNESCO World Heritage waterside Bryggen district. It was one of those beautiful moments, but with something missing. I was alone and couldn't share the experience with my loved ones. Nothing unusual there, I suppose. Get used to it, boy!

I just skipped past a railway. Apologies to the rail aficionados reading this. The Fløibanen is a lovely tourist funicular connecting the heart of Bergen's Fish Market wharf with the mountain station of Mount Fløyen. In less than 1km the two cars climb to 320 metres above sea level. The views from the top are well worth the price of the ticket and those with more energy than I had at that point in the day, plus some more daylight to play with, can use this as the start point of an invigorating mountain walk.

Back home it was Mothers' Day. By sheer fortune, with so much travel in my life, I had never missed a big moment like a first smile, a first word or first steps. I planned my trips generally midweek to make sure I was home every weekend and, of course, I never missed a significant date. This trip needed a weekend, however, and I somehow hadn't factored in Mothers' Day. With a five year old and a three year old at home, a plot was formed. A tray was hidden under the stairs with lots of goodies. A bottle of ice tea would be the safe replacement for a cuppa, the croissants would have to be served cold out of a wrapper, the flower wouldn't be a real one. With the girls' cards added by Erin and the tray duly delivered for breakfast, hopefully the cute surprise would be better and more touching than if I had been there? That was my hope, anyway.

Bergen, Norway's second city, is a lovely place, particularly along the Bryggen waterfront, where the wharf is flanked on one side by a stunning collection of Hanseatic merchant buildings so remarkable that they form a UNESCO protected World Heritage site. Bobbing around both sides of the quay visiting hotels, I paused for a good lunch opportunity. At the quayside was a van selling locally caught fish and chips in newspaper, a relatively cheap meal by Norwegian standards at £15, although this was admittedly nearly ten years ago. Fish. Chips. Newspaper. Fifteen chuffing quid! Gulp.

My favourite hotel was not the most plush, but had character and history. The Grand Hotel Terminus, as the name suggests, is planted across the road from Bergen's train station. Yes, I know I'm biased and, yes, I do love railway hotels. This one is a national protected building, built in 1928. On the wall of the wood panelled whisky bar is a photograph of the hotel's most celebrated guest, Roald Amundsen, who planned his last expedition from that very spot. Plotting my next expedition from the bar at Amundsen's former nerve centre, I hoped it wouldn't be my last!

The Bergen Railway is Norway's great long-distance train journey. Described as a journey 'across the roof of Norway', northern Europe's highest altitude train line departs Bergen around midday, climbing through rugged mountains via a series of tunnels blasted through the rocks, the longest of which is the Trollkona Tunnel at over five miles in length. Despite being the end of winter and beginning of spring, deep snow (and I mean several feet of deep snow!) surrounded the track as we ascended into a wilderness high above the tree line. The lonely station building at Myrdal is notable as the mountain terminus of the Flåm Railway, that other great Norwegian railway experience. Soon afterwards we reach the highest station on the line at Finse, some 4,267 feet (1,303 metres) above sea level, before the line descends over 3,000 feet within the next 60 miles, crossing through the beautiful Hallingdal Valley and the ski resort of Geilo, before reaching lush, fertile pastures so contrasting to the line's earlier barren beauty. Truly one of the great railway journeys.

Norwegian trains, long-distance ones anyway, are smart. Whilst the standard of NSB's trains may not compare favourably with the unmatchable Swiss rail experience, the scenery is arguably just as good. Seating in standard class is comfortable and service is good too. As I mentioned earlier, whilst there is an opportunity to upgrade to a small first class carriage, I'd suggest that the supplement isn't really worth it for a leather seat, a cup of coffee and a Norwegian language newspaper.

Journey's end was Oslo some seven hours later. Tired from my journey and settling into my room in a hotel thankfully just 50 metres from Oslo Sentralstation, I put on my jimjams, found an English language film and did a rare thing for me. I opened the minibar, fancying a glass of wine to wind down at the end of my trip. £15 for a small bottle. Gulp. 'Tapwater it is then!' I muttered to myself. Actually, I probably said, 'tapwatter' in my best South Yorkshire accent, followed by, 'how much?!' It dawned on me why those locals at the start of this chapter were emptying Duty Free as if there were no tomorrow. Now I know why Norwegian artist Edvard Munch's 'The Scream' painting was screaming; he had seen the price of a beer! Whilst it had been a sober trip, what a place it is, with lovely cities, connected by long-distance journeys through a natural beauty almost indescribable, plus a real coastal adventure without the razzmatazz. To paraphrase Bjørge Lillelien, Norway takes some beating. I'd recommend booking an inclusive tour for better value, with included meals negotiated into the hotel contracts by someone like me. We'd better get saving those pennies then, folks!

Chapter 15 - No! Sleep! Til Brooklyn! New York, Chicago & Washington DC

'**M**r Carroll, if you try to bring your groups to my hotel I will simply walk them straight back out of the door!'
The new manager of our new hotel in Washington DC was in a combative mood on the phone. A contract had been signed by his predecessor, but he would only honour the contract if we agreed to pay nearly double the rate. The groups were sold out, all 40 of them. He was threatening to tear up the agreement and send transatlantic guests back out onto the street.

'Sir, I think it's time we met in person,' I responded. 'I'll see you next week.'

Flights were booked and an itinerary that would make the most out of a transatlantic trip, but would either end in fisticuffs or a new 'special relationship'.

Arriving at JFK, most people would opt for an easy airport transfer straight to their hotel. Not me though. I opted for the public transport way to Manhattan. Well, what did you expect?! First up is the Air Train from the airport to Jamaica station, which connects with the New York subway and the Long Island Railroad. I decided to take the Long Island Railroad, whose termini conjure up exciting images for this lone traveller. Rockaway Beach was a track on the Ramones album 'Rocket to Russia' from 1977 in the heyday of punk. I couldn't get Ramones songs out of my head through my short stays in New York. Babylon, on the other hand, conjured up a completely different image. But my train would take me in the opposite direction through Queens and towards Manhattan, finally catching the subway at Penn Station for my hotel in the then recently gentrified Upper West Side, just round the corner from Central Park.

It was Saturday evening. For my sins I support FC St Pauli, a very mediocre German second division football team. Actually, that year was one of our few and far between one season stints in the top flight. There is a fan club in New York and that evening they would be showing our game against SC Freiburg at their headquarters, a bar in Williamsburg, Brooklyn. They show the game via internet stream, in full but after the match has finished, as if it were live, avoiding all social media that might give away the score. It was a slightly bizarre way to begin the trip, drinking Radeberger Premium Pils (a beer from Saxony) with a dozen or so German ex-pats and interested New Yorkers, watching a poor quality, buffering stream of a game half a world away that had already finished a couple of hours ago. But I enjoyed it so much that I came home and helped set up something very similar in Leeds. We are still going strong. Stronger than St Pauli at any rate, who are still very mediocre, on the pitch at least.

It's strong stuff that Radeberger, or maybe my brain fuzz was not helped by the weariness of a transatlantic flight. All I know is that after the game (it finished 1-1) I stepped onto the subway and got out in Manhattan at what I thought would be the right station. I was very wrong. Very Very wrong. How cool is it though that in New York all you need to be able to do, if you happen to be slightly, ahem, inebriated, is to count up to 74 to get home. My hotel was at 74th and Broadway. Oh, and maybe you also need to be prepared to walk a few miles if you find yourself somehow at 8th Street! But what a way for New York City to introduce itself, as I counted the blocks through Greenwich Village late Saturday night, past the Flatiron Building, the Empire State Building in the distance, then past Macy's to the kaleidoscope of colour that is Times Square. By the time I reached the Columbus Circle, the remaining 15 blocks seemed to drag and I was happy to sneak gingerly into bed.

Sunday morning Upper West Side. After my first encounter with a diner for breakfast, I went off to view a couple of hotels that had been willing to meet me. It was Sunday after all. Filling time, I took a cruise on the Hudson River to the Statue of Liberty, then under the Brooklyn and Williamsburg Bridges on the East River to the United Nations Building. It's a great way to see the sights, from the Empire State Building to the (for me anyway) more impressive Art Deco Chrysler Building.

AMTRAK train 49 leaves New York's Penn Station mid-afternoon. The route is called Lake Shore Limited and it begins an evening journey northwards through New York State through towns like Poughkeepsie, Albany, Schenectady and Syracuse. Through the night the train heads westwards via Buffalo to Cleveland, through Ohio and Indiana to Illinois, arriving in Chicago after breakfast mid-morning 959 miles later. That's the plan anyway.

AMTRAK sleeper compartments are probably the most comfortable that I've experienced. You will have gathered by now that I'm not a fan, generally, of travelling overnight as I just can't sleep, but needs must if you want to cross this vast continent by train. That said, I like the AMTRAK experience. If you aren't in a hurry, it's a great way to get to know America. For those in sleepers, your private cabin has facing seats that are pulled down together in the evening to become your bed. There's an upper bunk too. Facilities are down the corridor. Meals are included on-board for passengers occupying sleeper accommodations. It's a sociable experience, as you tend to share a table in the restaurant car, whilst a hearty meal is served. The same thing happens at breakfast too. The train staff seem more like fellow travellers and it takes a certain type of person to work these routes; the lifestyle of constant long-distance travel has to suit you. With one of two of the crew you got the feeling that this life on the road (or, more correctly, on the rails) was an escape from a previous life.

I'd recommend AMTRAK as a means of seeing America for anyone with time to spare, whether visiting long lost relatives or travelling on holiday. It's maybe not the best mode of transport for those travelling on business though. I had scheduled my trip to arrive in Chicago just after 9am on Monday morning, leaving Chicago again on a different

AMTRAK sleeper just after 6pm the same day bound for Washington DC on the Capitol Limited train. A punishing schedule to say the least for someone generally unable to sleep on trains, but, hey, you need a sense of adventure in this job, right?!

I had arranged meetings with 6 or 8 hotels around Chicago's Magnificent Mile. One thing I haven't mentioned about AMTRAK, however, is that passenger services are often hit by long delays to allow the easy passage of freight traffic, which takes precedence in the States. By the time we rolled into Chicago after midday I had already cancelled four appointments, much to the distaste of the hoteliers concerned.

Chicago I will deal with in another chapter on a subsequent trip when I stayed more than 4 or 5 hours. Music follows me around my visits to the States though and my short visit to Chicago was no different, with the scraping metallic noise of Steve Albini's post-punk band Big Black echoing in the screech of the brakes from the Chicago Loop trains rattling above your head on this late winter's day.

I was soon enough back at Chicago Union Station, bag checked in, sitting in the waiting room ahead of the second successive overnight journey with AMTRAK. This one would take me to Washington DC, home of some of my American punk rock musical heroes, Minor Threat, Bad Brains and Fugazi.

I saw Fugazi play a benefit gig at Leeds Polytechnic back in 1989. It was for a great cause and there were three bands on the bill. The first was the wonderfully named Thatcher on Acid. They were followed by local heroes Chumbawamba, who you might know had a massive hit with 'Tubthumping'. You'll know it if you hear it, with the lyrics 'I get knocked down, but I get up again. You're never gonna keep me down.' It was the third and headline band Fugazi that I was there to see though, fronted by two legends of this admittedly obscure scene that I liked in my snotty days of youth. Ian MacKaye was the former lead singer of Minor Threat, one of my favourite punk bands and leaders of the 'Straight Edge' movement that frowned on drink, drugs, promiscuity and machismo. Guy Picciotto was from another seminal band, Rites of Spring, arguably the first ever Emo band (you might need to ask your kids!). Thatcher on Acid played and went, Chumbawamba played, played some more, took a breather for a raffle to be drawn, played on, played some more, went off again, came back on, got knocked down, got up again, played some more.... Would they ever leave the goddamn stage? Finally, finally Ian MacKaye strode on to announce that there was a curfew in place, that they only had 30 minutes left to play, then proceeded to rip through a Fugazi set at a visceral breakneck pace that good old AMTRAK cannot ever match. I will never forget it.

The Capitol Limited train runs 764 miles from early evening Chicago, via night-time stops in Pittsburgh and Cleveland, through morning in Maryland and West Virginia to the District of Columbia. The route follows the historic Baltimore & Ohio line on a journey through the Allegheny Mountains, the Potomac Valley and past historic Harpers Ferry, arriving into Washington DC Union Station at just after 1pm in the afternoon.

Back to the real business and my reason for being in DC, I had four hotels to see that afternoon, including some down by the Dupont Circle and in Georgetown, two young, lively and trendy neighbourhoods. The meeting with the combative hotelier who wanted to throw 40 groups back out onto the street was scheduled for the following morning. This afternoon was my chance to find a plan B. Between the hotel I was staying that night and a few other possibilities, maybe I could house all 40 groups elsewhere and deliver the ultimate punk rock gesture of a two-finger salute to my opponent the following day. My final hotel in Georgetown was the one hotel that I knew could take all 40 groups. I had high hopes, but they were soon shattered in a strange stench. It was a pet-friendly hotel. The first room had a funny smell. In the second it was more intense. I so wanted the third room not to stink but, yes, it reeked and the stench was definitely wee. Doggy wee, to be precise. I'm an animal lover and we've always had pets, but one room nearly made me vom on the spot. I remember thinking to myself, 'If these are the rooms they are showing me, what the hell are the others like?!' It would be like sleeping in the stairwell of a multi-storey car park, something I have experienced and wouldn't wish on my customers! But would they end up on a Washington DC street?!

Back at my sweeter smelling hotel for the night, just a block away from the problem hotel, I ended my day being shown round by its manager. It was a good alternative but they couldn't take all the dates.

As it drew to a close something strange came over me. Back then I put it down to two consecutive sleepless nights on AMTRAK trains, plus running around like a blue arsed fly as usual. With hindsight it was my body telling me I was weak, there was something wrong and that it needed attention. It would take a few more years of constant travel, plus a more dramatic episode in a hotel up a mountain, before I would get the medical advice needed. But back then, visibly shaking with some kind of fever (or fatigue), I managed to make a professional exit from the situation, slid into bed fully-clothed, with the robe from the bathroom on too, under the quilt, still shaking like a leaf with a chill I didn't understand. How the hell was I going to combat Mr Angry Hotelier the following day?

Twelve hours later I awoke fully-clothed, gowned, somewhat confused but remarkably fit for purpose. Suited and booted (though I decided against the steel toe-capped Docs as I was aiming for more charm than harm), I headed round the corner to see my adversary, the main reason for this trip. It's amazing, the power of meeting someone in person, speaking to their face, rather down a phone line or email. Hidden deep beneath this silent and sullen Yorkshireman there are a couple of characters I let out only occasionally. One is the Hugh Grant-type hapless but vaguely charming Englishman, which is reserved for female Italian Police officers threatening me with a fine for driving through a red light. The other is more old-school David Niven. I say, old chap!

How could anyone sit there and throw charming David Niven's 40 lovely groups out onto the street? He couldn't, of course. We reached a compromise that kept all the groups in his hotel and at the originally agreed rate. Actually, that's not a compromise, is it? Still, fair's fair, old chap, and thanks for being such a good sport.

Washington DC is an eerie town. I liked the buzzing quarters populated by students and young people, but the downtown has a real transient feel. The buildings are, of course, stately and there are big institutions here, but by its very nature DC is a city populated by people in transit, moving to the city, or in and out of town, purely for work.

Back on a train then, mission accomplished, this time on an AMTRAK daytime service taking me up the Northeast corridor. My trip would end back where it started in New York City. There are several options actually, as it's also possible to take a seat on one of AMTRAK's long-distance services, such as 'The Crescent' which originates in New Orleans, but the commuter train option throws up two possibilities. The 'Acela' is the faster service, at 2 hours 50 minutes between the two cities. I opted for the slower 'Northeast Regional', connecting Washington DC Union Station with New York Penn in 3 hours 20 minutes. Travel slower, folks. You get to see more.

Okay, I was putting myself in our customers' shoes, as they would be on the slower service away from the hardcore commuters. Plus, the slower train stopped at what appeared to be my very own station, New Carrollton, Maryland. New Carrollton, in reality, seemed as unassuming and unremarkable as its namesake. Then came Baltimore, which reminded me of home as we trundled through. Home as in hard northern industrial towns. Philadelphia was up next, a place I vowed to make a stop next time, before we eventually made it back into Penn, right at the heart of New York City.

On a work trip where you spend your time racing between cities (well, racing as fast as AMTRAK can muster), then racing between hotels within those cities, any personal sightseeing can only be done after dark. I guess I've become an expert on many cities post-twilight. What a city Manhattan is after darkness falls. I had to go and have a look at Greenwich Village, Christopher Street in particular. It was here that the Stonewall Riots happened in 1969, outside the Stonewall Inn to be precise, arguably the birth of the gay rights movement and still iconic to this day.

Then there's the Chelsea Hotel, long-term lodging of writers, poets, artists, philosophers and musicians. The list is as long as a very long arm. The beat poets, such as Allen Ginsberg, used to meet here to exchange ideas. Dylan Thomas was staying here when he was found ill, succumbing to pneumonia. The alternative history of the alternative hotel then took an even more gruesome twist when Nancy Spungen, girlfriend of Sex Pistol Sid Vicious, was found stabbed to death in her room. Madonna lived at the Chelsea in the 80s and returned to shoot photos for her book, 'Sex'.

Then on the Bower there's also CBGBs, which stands for 'Country, Bluegrass and Blues', but a club forever entwined with the New York punk and New Wave scene, where the Ramones, Patti Smith, Blondie and Talking Heads cut their teeth. It closed in 2006 and is now a fashion retailer, a sad but inevitable part of the gentrification in the neighbourhood.

The following day would be my last on this trip, racing around no less than ten hotels on a busy New York day. I did manage an early morning stroll through Central Park and to the Dakota Building, where John Lennon lived and was shot. Of course I also managed time out at a cathedral of rail travel, the awe inspiring Central Station.

'Up to Lexington, one, two, five....I'm waiting for my man.' But, unlike Lou Reed, the man I was waiting for was the Sales Manager of the Radisson Lexington Avenue. The Ramones song about New York's scuzzy side, '53rd and 3rd', buzzed through my head the whole day. But New York, Manhattan anyway, is a different animal to Lou Reed's city or the Ramones' version. It's the safest I've ever felt, as a lone traveller, in any US city. Okay, so I didn't take a walk on the wild side, but New York became one of my favourite places. This chapter has had a bit of a punk rock soundtrack in my head, so let's bring it to a close with the calmer craft of another native New Yorker, Billy Joel. Nope, it's not about uptown girls or denying all knowledge of starting fires. I'm in a New York state of mind.

Chapter 16 - Caledonia Dreaming Part 5

B ack in the day there was a little railway on the Isle of Mull. The Scottish islands' only line, it was not surprisingly called the Isle of Mull Railway. Running on a tiny 10 ¼ inch track the little locos pulled their loads 1 ¼ miles from Caledonian MacBrayne's Craignure ferry terminal to Torosay Castle, also well worth a visit. That was until 2010, when the castle was put up for sale and a decision taken that running a railway through the land may not be viable if the new owner did not wish for the estate to be open to the public. Thus the track was lifted and one of Mull's attractions disappeared for good. Steam locos Frances, Victoria and Glen Auldyn are now located at the charming Rudyard Lake Railway in Staffordshire, in case you fancy a hint of what the Isle of Mull Railway was like.

A little Staffordshire side-story here, naming a newborn baby after the place where it was conceived did not start with the Beckhams. Did you know that the author Rudyard Kipling's parents enjoyed their courtship beside the Rudyard Lake so much that they named their son after the 2 ½ mile long man-made reservoir near Leek, a very lovely local beauty spot? It could have been worse for the boy, Rudyard, I suppose. His school days could have been so much more difficult. Had his parents courted by the lake at the other side of town he would have been called Tittesworth.

Oh dear. Is this a travel book or a 'Carry On' film? Where was I? Ah, yes, the Isle of Mull. My mind wandered a little there. Mull is a small place, everyone knows everyone else's business and so when Torosay Castle closed to the public, with the subsequent closure of the little railway, a knight in shining armour headed over the hill. Well, actually, he headed over Duart Bay and he was the Chieftain.

Yes, that's correct, the Chieftain. Not that he called himself the Chieftain. The phone just rang one day and on the other end of the line was Lachy. If we were stuck, with nowhere to go from Craignure and no coach, he had a coach, would pick up our groups from the ferry for a tour of Duart Castle and open the tea rooms for refreshments. Duart is the ancestral home of the Clan Maclean and Lachy is Sir Lachlan Maclean of Duart and Morven, 12th Baronet of Nova Scotia and 28th chief of Clan Maclean.

By now I didn't just travel regularly to Scotland with work. We would also head up there probably once a year on holiday too. Not too long after that phone call we went on a family trip in the western Highlands, inevitably enjoying parts of my tours on an Easter trip glowing with an unusually kind sun. In Fort William we had soared to the top of Aonach Mor on the Nevis Range Mountain Gondola, the only one of its kind in Britain and reaching an altitude of 650 metres on the north face of Britain's 8th highest mountain. Built to transport skiers, there was still skiing taking places on the slopes at the top, where instead we gingerly sauntered across the precarious ice to the playground so the kids could see-saw and swing whilst we gazed below at the crisp clarity of the Nevis Range on such an incredibly clear March morning.

From Fort William we would drive to Oban for the ferry to Mull, with a detour at Connel. At this unassuming pebble beach we had scattered mum's ashes. It was a perfect day to reflect, the sun illuminating the waves, the wet pebbles shining warmth into our sad hearts. We would then hop up the Isle of Mull to one of its other ferry ports, ending the day on the Ardnamurchan Peninsula at Scotland's and mainland Britain's westernmost point.

The Sound of Mull was a millpond as the ferry skidded away from Oban. We gently passed Lismore, the island we'd also gazed at from Connel. From Craignure on Mull we approached Duart, stopping again and again to photograph the castle in the distance across the fields. At

Duart we got an unexpected surprise. Our groups' usual guide came to meet us, a lovely chap called Andrew.

'I'm not taking you round. Your guide today is the Chief.'

Then Lachy appeared, a gentle and benevolent man in his late 60s at the time, with an unassuming air, a dress sense that screamed slightly eccentric aristocrat, but a man full of natural warmth and charm. The kids were young, so we had to have a little word in their ears when Lachy wasn't looking.

'This bloke isn't a tour guide, even though that's how it seems. This castle is his house. He's like the king of the island. So, behave yourselves, otherwise we might get kicked off!'

I have never met royalty and never particularly wanted to. The closest I came was at a German Tourist Board press conference launching the 300th anniversary of the Hanoverian succession to the British crown in 2014. We were told to bow or curtsey when Prince Ernst August of Hanover entered the room. I would not bow to anyone, let alone a prince from a dynasty that ended in 1918. What's more, I was a tad disappointed. I had only gone along under the impression that I was meeting Ernst August, husband of Princess Caroline of Monaco, the bad boy prince, the one caught by tabloids peeing in the street and generally being a bit of an embarrassing drunk. Instead, they rolled out his son, also Ernst August, a charming and likeable young man, an ambassador that would do any family or country proud, but slightly less exciting.

Lachy, Chief of Clan Maclean, was my children's king for the day. What a lovely guy and what a surprise to us all. Speaking of surprises, I had promised the kids a surprise that day. As we drove northwards on this 'Scotland in Miniature' style island, rumours spread across the back seat. Would the surprise be McDonalds perhaps?

McDonalds? On the Isle of Mull? There are only Macleans around here. As we approached the brightly coloured houses on Tobermory's attractive harbour front it all became clear, memories of their recent infant television favourite, Balamory.

Clocking up another thousand or so miles of driving around Scotland, Mrs C decided to let me have a surprise of my own. She would drive the couple of hundred yards from Tobermory to its ferry terminal, then the few hundred yards from the other side to our hotel in Kilchoan. My treat for all my driving? Whilst they went off in search of Miss Hooley, Josey Jump, Pocket & Sweet, and Archie the Inventor, I would get own personal tour of Tobermory Distillery, followed by a tasting. As it transpired, the boss himself took me round and into a small tasting room at the end. Okay, maybe he wasn't the Chieftain of the Malt, but he was the General Manager at least and he kept miraculously producing rare malts from under the counter. So much so that when I emerged into the March late afternoon bright daylight, slightly, erm, well, let's just say I needed sunglasses and a bit of help to the car. Slàinte.

Chapter 17 - Bangkok to Singapore

Τhis chapter begins with your sole traveller a bag of nerves wearing a shirt he wouldn't normally be seen dead in at Bangkok's Suvarnabhumi Airport. Thailand operated unusual visa regulations. A visa was required to enter the country to work, but not as a tourist. It had been a relatively hastily arranged trip and I hadn't bothered to get a visa, opting instead to hunt through the local charity shops in my town for a suitably loud holiday shirt to hoodwink the Thai border officials. The almost-Hawaiian shirt would be discarded at the first hotel (honest!). Deary me, how to turn a simple work trip into something akin to a Cold War spy thriller. Well, not quite, but that's how it felt in my fertile imagination for those few moments queuing to enter. After all, if it didn't work this could be a costly and embarrassing mistake.

I made it through. Phew. And my smiling Bangkok guide, Kingkarn, was waiting at the other side to transport me to my first hotel, an opulent international 5* tower overlooking the Chao Phraya river. The remainder of the day was recovery, ahead of a full-on week piecing together a new tour that would take in Thailand, Malaysia and Singapore, the route of the Eastern Oriental luxury train, but using the state railways. I needed to check out the suitability (or unsuitability) of the trains, whilst choosing hotels and attractions to visit along the route.

To explain the route, after the following day in Bangkok I would take the sleeper train north to Chiangmai. After a day and night in

Chiangmai I would take the long daytime train back to Bangkok. The following morning I'd take a flight from Bangkok to Penang in Malaysia. After a day there I'd continue by train from Butterworth to Kuala Lumpur. Then, after a night in KL, I'd continue by train to Singapore for a couple of nights before flying home.

So, it would be an early start the next day, touring Bangkok's hotels and sights, and I was feeling slightly weird. Was it evening? Well, yes. Should I try to sleep? Well, how? So I went in search of something that might encourage rest. Rice wine would do the trick, surely?

On my way back from the Seven Eleven I peered into the many tailor shop windows. Suits made to measure in 24 hours. Interesting. Bearing in mind the fact that I would be returning to Bangkok in a couple of days, maybe I could get myself measured up, collect in a couple of days and return home with a new jacket. The sports jacket in one window looked tempting, with a pleasing green in the check. Rather nice, I thought, so in I went to enquire and barter with the tailor. If nothing else it would hone my negotiation skills a little ahead of the hotel meetings. Sadly it ended with an impasse, a gulf between us, the tailor and me, of about £5. Neither of us would budge and I was too stubborn to cave in. So off I toddled out of the shop, with no promise of a made-to-measure sports jacket with a pleasing green tinge in the check......whooooooa....hold on a minute!! What the hell was going on there?! I hadn't even had a sip of rice wine yet. Let's repeat the words....made-to-measure....sports jacket....with a pleasing green tinge in the check. Was this the precise moment when I became middle-aged?! A chuffing sports jacket?! Pleasing green tinge in the chuffing check?! Punk's not dead.....he just now wants to dress like his dad....or his grandad!

So the newly-affirmed middle-aged man didn't venture far that evening. I sipped my rice wine by my umpteenth floor window, watching the boats come and go up and down the Chao Phraya until I nodded off. Bangkok could wait until the next day.

Bangkok is a city rammed with life and colour, but it would have to wait a little while longer. My new day started with the important job of sussing out hotels for our eventual tour. I was taken from one opulent western-style tower to the next. I could have been in any city, but I suppose that's the comfort blanket westerners require when sampling a tiny bit of a very different culture.

My whistle-stop taster of Bangkok's cultural tapestry came in the afternoon with visits to its most important temples. Wat Pho is the Temple of the Reclining Buddha, at 46 metres long a chilled-out giant in gold plate, apart from its feet which are adorned instead with mother of pearl. Close by is the 61 acre Royal Palace, a kaleidoscope of golden spires, temples and shrines. Within the palace grounds is Wat Phra Kaew, the Temple of the Emerald Buddha. This most important Buddhist temple in Thailand dates from the 15th century, the Buddha carved into a 66 cm tall block of jade. Nobody is allowed near it except the king and strict dress code applies. Finally, Wat Traimit, the Temple of the Golden Buddha boasts the world's largest solid gold statue, a seated Buddha at five metres in height. After my guide Kingkarn insisted on taking a photo of his slightly embarrassed guest in front of the Golden Buddha, we hotfooted it to the next nearby temple, a temple of the railways, Bangkok's Hua Lamphong station.

There were and are several means of reaching Chiangmai in the north of the country, both on daytime trains and sleeper services. I had decided to take the sleeper northwards, returning on the daytime train in order to try out both options. In truth I had done my research and had already decided I wouldn't feature the sleeper train in the tour I was designing. At this juncture I need to say that since my visit new Chinese trains have been introduced with more modern facilities, but at that time there was only a limited number of First Class sleeper compartments, certainly not enough to accommodate a group, and these were basic by European standards. For the majority the sleeper experience was more communal and, feeling adventurous, I had decided not to pay the small upgrade (for westerners) to First Class, opting instead for the real authentic local rail experience that, of course, I wouldn't dream of unleashing on paying customers.

Hua Lamphong's ornate façade was designed by an Italian architect in neo-Renaissance style, based on Frankfurt Hauptbahnhof and opened in 1916. Sleeper train no 9 departs just after 6pm. All is as per a normal daytime train journey for the first part of the trip until the attendants arrive to push opposing seats together, turning them into a lower berth. A narrower upper berth (the cheapest option) pulls down from the wall. Curtains are then pulled across, turning a normal everyday train carriage into makeshift semi-private sleeper compartments. Across the aisle from my lower berth was a middle-aged German couple. The husband had booked the tickets and, unlike me, evidently he hadn't done his research. His wife was not happy. My Thai seating companion, by contrast, was used to the scenario, settled into the top bunk and was out like a light judging from the snores. For me, yet another sleepless night on a sleeper train. Needs must sometimes, but if you are someone who struggles to sleep, then you are better to travel during the day when you can see the scenery, before climbing into a hotel bed to actually have some shut-eye. The train chugged through the night across landscapes I would see in daylight a couple of days later, my companion dreamed his dreams on the top bunk and the German woman bemoaned her husband's slack planning. Western problems. It was an admittedly small price to pay for an adventure, but

I was already looking forward to collapsing into a hotel bed, though I would have to wait 24 hours for that luxury.

Emerging from Chiangmai station early the following morning at around 7.30am, bleary-eyed and into the bright sunshine, this was another place entirely. Now up in lush mountainous terrain, Chiangmai is a large city but with a much more laidback feel, clearly appealing to tourists seeking something else after Bangkok's breakneck pace. The Shangri La Hotel allowed me to check in early, but alas it was just to drop my bag. Boy, did that bed look inviting, but my smiling and eager guide was waiting to show me around another five or six very similar luxurious hotels, before sampling some of the sights that might make it into the final itinerary. Blimey.

The hotels I was shown were the height of luxury, including an extraordinary out-of-town 5* resort with individual villas with their own individual spas. An orchid farm was next on the agenda, where we could walk amidst the most exquisite of flowers, a certain inclusion for the eventual tour itinerary. Our final stop was not so clear cut though. I was looking forward to visiting an elephant camp and seeing elephants close-up. The mahouts (tenders) didn't appear to mistreat the elephants, but the visit turned into a bit of a circus that didn't sit comfortably with me. I suppose the gentle giants were bound to have a game of football for the onlooking tourist crowd, but the final trick was for Nelly to sit at an easel, hold a paint brush in her trunk and paint a picture to sell to the awestruck tourists. I could only imagine how that particular skill had been 'trained' into the poor elephants for our benefit and left the camp feeling guilty on behalf of my industry. Later, as darkness fell, outside my hotel was an interesting night market in which you could buy a fake version of virtually every western brand, but in truth, it wasn't as interesting as my lovely hotel bed, particularly as the following day would be spent on board a train back to Bangkok. Nighty night.

The daytime train of choice would be the Diesel Railcar Express, departing Chiangmai at around 8am, arriving back in Bangkok at around 7.30pm. Carriages are Second Class only, but with reclining seats and ceiling fans acting as air-conditioning. Included in the fare were refreshments and a rice lunch, which were very welcome. Leaving aside the toilets, which reminded me of some of the (in)conveniences I have experienced at non-league football grounds or basement rock clubs, it was a reasonably comfortable experience, with scenery constantly changing outside the window through landscapes as diverse as soaring peaks and verdant tropical forests. The first part of the journey heads down through mountainous country, gaining an insight into rural Thai life, stopping at a selection of rustic hillside communities, with farmers hard at work on their agricultural plains, tranquil backwaters of rice fields and with the occasional golden temple visible from the train. Halting at tiny rural stations, locals would get on and off, usually with a proud stationmaster in pristine uniform ready with flag to signal our journey onwards towards the capital.

This time we were delayed and my arrival was at around 9pm, a full 13 hours after the journey had started. Tired, but hungry from the journey, I dumped my bag back in the hotel room and headed towards the humble restaurant across the road from the hotel. A taxi driver caught me before I could go in.

'Taxi sir? I'll take you to where all the restaurants are?'

'No thanks. I'm going to that one,' I replied, pointing to the one directly a few feet in front of me.

'That one will be closing now. Jump in. I'll take you to a really good restaurant.'

I only wanted something to eat before crawling into bed, so ignored my cabbie friend. But just as I was about to push the handle, the door to the restaurant was locked for the night. Tail now firmly between my legs, tummy rumbling as well, I had to walk past the taxi driver again.

'So,' he said grinning a very smug grin, 'jump in!'

'No thanks. I'm tired. I'm getting room service,' was the honest response from this stubborn-as-a-mule Yorkshireman.

'How long are you staying in Bangkok?' asked my persistent new-found buddy.

When I told him it would be just one night, he produced a laminated A4 piece of paper decorated with photos of young women.

'You have one night in Bangkok and you are spending it alone?! Come on, tell me which one you would like?'

When I wearily told him I wasn't interested he pulled out another laminated A4 piece of paper, this time decorated with photos of boys or young men.

'Aaaah,' said he, giving me a knowing wink, 'I see, well, how about one of these?'

When I finally dodged the cabbie to cross the road to the sanity of my hotel room, behind me I heard the same voice concerning himself that I seemed stressed and, of course, offering to sell me a calming joint. This was a truly unique moment in my travelling life, to be offered a taxi ride, a meal, a female prostitute, a male prostitute and drugs, all at the same time from a mobile one-stop-sex-and-drugs-shop. This was also the only time in my travelling life when I have ordered room service. In my safe western-style luxury hotel, watching the lights of the boats bobbing up and down the Chao Phraya river.

Through Malaysia to Singapore

For the next leg of the journey southwards I cheated. I had no intention of putting our customers on a sleeper train through Thailand's deep south into Malaysia, mainly due to lack of comfort, but also for safety reasons. The Foreign Office advised at the time against all but essential travel through certain border provinces due to insurgencies (since revoked). Equally, I didn't have the stomach for another rocky night in a curtained-off bed in a normal train carriage, accompanied by the snores of fellow travellers and maybe a bickering German couple. Instead I flew with budget airline Air Asia from Bangkok to Penang, an island off Malaysia's west coast.

Maybe the concept of budget airlines as we know them in Europe hadn't translated well to Asia. You know, the idea of stripping out every single item we would have once expected as part of the package, then sneeringly re-selling them individually back to us as add-ons. Not so with Air Asia, it would seem. Instead of contempt I was met with pleasant, smiling and helpful cabin crew and served a meal that was included in the fare. Service and value for money? What a refreshing change!

Landing in Penang, my new guide whisked me to an Indian canteen up in the hills before dropping me at my small and friendly boutique hotel in Georgetown, the island's main city. Georgetown is an interesting mix of cultures and styles, with grand colonial architecture from its time as a British territory contrasting with vibrant, colourful Chinese influences, with a little piece of India thrown into the melting pot for good measure.

The Eastern & Oriental Hotel in Georgetown was a must visit place and should have been the perfect base for the clientele for whom I was researching the tour, but it left me a little cold. Founded by the Sarkies Brothers, the hoteliers of Armenian descent who went on to found Raffles Hotel in Singapore (more of which later!), the gleaming white hotel is built in a British colonial style that many would find pleasing, but, that colonial feeling...maybe that was the problem for me. I wasn't in search of empire; I was putting a tour together. Elsewhere, the centre of Georgetown is a UNESCO World Heritage Site with varied landmarks portraying its cultural mix, including an Anglican church, a Chinese temple, an Indian temple and the Kapitan Kelling Mosque.

Do we base the tour in bustling Georgetown or along the coast at a relaxed resort called Batu Ferringhi was the next question? To find the answer we headed west to view multiple luxurious western-style resort hotels and I spent a night there. The gulf between rich and poor was very noticeable, with holiday palaces on one side of the street and shacks on the other. One particular hotel sales manager was heavily pregnant. I really mean it; she was ready to burst. I was curious to find out when her baby was due.

'Next week,' came her response.

My mind whirred at the thought of the woman in front of me working until her waters broke. I sheepishly asked when she would return to work after the birth.

'The following week.'

I was gobsmacked. When I was about to become a dad for the first time I had asked my old boss about paternity leave. 'You are very lucky, son. Here at Wallace Arnold you get up to three days paternity leave....as long as they are Saturday, Sunday...and Bank Holiday Monday!' That had been a clever (if facetious) joke, whereas this short interaction with a smart sales manager in a swish hotel provided the latest culture quake to my naïve western mind.

The next day would be a long one, beginning with a transfer to the port, a ferry to the mainland, then my first experience of Malaysian rail from Butterworth to Kuala Lumpur on the next leg of the epic journey south.

If Bangkok Hua Lamphong train station had been a railway cathedral and Chiangmai a quaint tropical paradise, then Butterworth was prosaic by comparison. Two miles from Georgetown across the Penang Strait, the town was named after a 19th century colonial governor. My rapid ferry dropped me next to the station and thankfully I didn't have long to wait. Early morning Butterworth felt like early morning Rotherham Central, but I believe the dilapidated old station has since been replaced with a spanking new modern building. Butterworth, I mean, not Rotherham.

I had booked a seat in First Class on the Malaysian Railways 'Ekspress' service. The trains were upgraded to much more modern units a few years later in 2015, but my journey began at around 7.30am in wide bucket seats reminiscent of AMTRAK trains in the USA, with ample legroom and good space, but a bit battered and unloved all the same. It was pleasant enough, trundling southwards along a single track towards Kuala Lumpur, but just one piece of advice I'd give is to take something woolly with you. Yes, outside is a tropical landscape of lushness, with thick forests, undulating hills and the Cameron Highlands in the distance, but when Malaysian Railways turn on the air-con boy do they crank it up.

Passengers alight at Ipoh for the Cameron Highlands, a tourist highlight of natural beauty and tea plantations. The next main conurbation is Kuala Lumpur itself, just after midday. KL is now served by the space-aged Sentral station and it's here that I left the train. My guide did, however, kindly take me to have a look at the city's monumental old station, a stunning edifice built in 1910 in Moorish-style.

An afternoon of hotel visits was punctuated by a peek inside Petaling Street Market in Chinatown, so awash with colour and aromas that I decided I'd return there during my limited free time after work.

Which I duly did. It seemed so simple, a relatively short walk (maybe a mile) from my little boutique hotel in a thriving, up-and-coming part of the city. Yes, I'd be able to spot that particular intersection on the return. No problem. Easy peasy.

Gifts duly bought at Petaling Street Market for my daughters, I decided to make my way back. How can I describe this? That feeling when you are alone in the centre of Kuala Lumpur, it's late and you are tired. And you realise you can't remember the name of your hotel. Or which district it is in. Or even which direction it's in. That feeling. Where was that intersection I had noted? All the roads looked the same. Everything I had, passport included, was at the hotel. Whose name and location I've forgotten. It was dark, I was tired, I looked very out of place and could very easily have wandered into danger.

Mild panic set in. It's still a mystery to me how I got back. The hotel was called Anggun and it's in Bukit Bintang, where big swish hotels and little private ones live side by side amongst lively streets, food stalls and the hullabaloo of city life. A good base for tourists. Tourists smart enough to make note of where they are staying, that is.

Back on Malaysian Railways' 'Ekspress' service the following early afternoon, this time with something woolly to combat extreme aircon, the single track southwards along the Malay Peninsula led to a mid-evening arrival in Singapore at the faded grandeur of Keppel Road's Singapore station, having negotiated the 1 km long causeway across the Johor Strait to the island. Sadly, this building and railway terminus was the subject of disputes after Malaysia and Singapore parted and, having wrestled the station and land from the control of the Malaysian government, the Singaporeans duly closed it, relocating to the workaday Woodlands Checkpoint on the north of the island. These days the journey I had just undertaken would end with a transfer or taxi rather than at the grand art-deco station. For a fast-growing financial superpower like Singapore this doesn't seem like progress.

Otherwise Singapore seemed indeed to be in a rich and gleaming state. It was how everyone describes it, spotlessly clean, oppressively humid. My hotel, the Fullerton, was named after another former colonial governor and had originally been the General Post Office. A short walk for a swift nightcap took me to Harry's Bar along the quayside, which was the favourite haunt of Nick Leeson, the rogue trader who brought down Barings Bank. In Singapore it's all about the money.

Singapore was a stark contrast to the previous week. A final day of hotel visits included the extraordinary Marina Bay Sands. You know, the one with three massive towers and the boat perched on the roof. Inside it's more like a shopping mall than a hotel, a bit clinical, which is a term you could use about Singapore in general. But that boat-shaped roof?! I hope you've got a head for heights! An infinity pool overlooks the city and you can see the ground seemingly miles below through little gaps in the wooden decking as you approach the ship's bow. My palms are sweating as I write this.

As the day was hotting up and to freshen up ahead of my flight home, a room had been made available for a few hours at the Fairmont Hotel. Peering out of my window, across the road I spied the famous

Raffles Hotel, that other institution founded by the Sarkies Brothers. I couldn't resist, so wandered across the road for a show-round at a hotel I could only dream of contracting, then slunk into a chair at the bar to order the hotel's world-famous cocktail, the Singapore Sling. Nowhere could I find the price. Would this famous drink in one of the world's most famous hotels cost me £1.50, £15 or £150? The answer would have to wait until the bill arrived. We Yorkshire folk are known to be spendthrift, so time for more sweaty palms! It was the middle one, by the way. Phew.

Chapter 18 - The Dam

'**Y**ou want some suckinandf**kin?'
I had just stepped out of Amsterdam Centraal station. Just that second. After a torrid night on an overnight ferry from Hull to Rotterdam, in those days (around 1996) a very popular route offering several standards of accommodation. With just a few brass farthings to rub together back then, I had chosen the lowest standard of 'accommodation', a reclining seat in a room with lots of other people. I hadn't slept on the seat, either upright or reclined, it also hadn't worked when I tried to sleep on the carpet under the seat. I had finally got to Amsterdam and within two seconds there's a guy jabbering profanities at me. Within the next hundred metres I was offered every possible sexual favour, every possible drug. Welcome to your holiday in Amsterdam! Great! Here we go again.

Thus began the worst holiday of my life. Well, actually it had gone downhill right from planning stage. My then girlfriend had spent some time chambermaiding at a hotel in the city. It had been a momentous period in her life, a start of a kind of adult freedom for her. And nearly every break we had in our short few years together featured 'The Dam'. The previous attempt had been a 'weekend break' with a local coach operator. Try to get your head around this one. You finish work Friday evening, join your coach and travel from Lancashire to Dover, then Calais to Amsterdam through the night. With no sleep, as I just cannot sleep on coaches or trains (or floors of ferries). Arriving at 6 o'clock in the morning you have the whole day in Amsterdam until midnight, a day visiting various coffee shops. At midnight (what day is it?) the journey home begins through the night to Calais, then Dover up to Lancashire, arriving home…god knows when…just in time to go back to work? Stinking. With two nights sleep-free on a stinking coach with a load of other stinking people and a mad 18 hours kicking your heels trying to experience freedom in Amsterdam's coffee shops. Jesus wept.

But that was the previous one. This one was for a whole week. We were doing it properly this time, staying in the youth hostel that had been her lodging for those halcyon days of her carefree years. My girlfriend worked in a typical Lancashire factory that operated 'wakes weeks', shutting down for a fortnight. That fortnight was your holiday, like it or lump it. The plan was for her to spend the first week in Amsterdam with her best friend, then the friend would go home and she would spend the second week with me. In the Christian youth hostel she had spoken so much about. In the middle of the Red Light District.

The interchange of companion after the first week was the key for me. You see, during my 50 years so far I've been pretty easy to befriend. I see the good bits in people and my shortlist of people I don't get on with is a very short shortlist. My then girlfiend's best friend was that shortlist. I had received a call a couple of days before the changeover was due to happen to break the news that she had decided to stay on another week. My week.

I made a quick call myself to my own best friend. 'Help me out, mate. Please come with me and keep me company.' And at short notice he did. We endured a night on the ferry carpet, somehow reached Amsterdam bleary eyed. 'We'll meet you outside the station,' she had said, but there was no welcome party apart from Mr Suckyf**ky and no address of this bloody 'Christian youth hostel in the Red Light District'.

Can I just point out that I am not religious in any way, shape or form. The Christian youth hostel was the cheapest place in town. You had to be there in person at 11am to book your bed for that night, otherwise you missed out, which explained the lack of welcome party. Rooms were large dorms, men in one and women in the other. I had a picture in my head of the other guests in the dorm: smart, side parting, freckles, bible in hand maybe? The reality was that none of the guys in our dorm adhered to my outdated and reactionary stereotype. Instead I was surrounded by young international middle-class youths, frazzled by constant days smoking weed in Amsterdam's coffee shops just because they could.

We somehow found the Christian Youth Hostel, the holiday began with a domestic exacerbated by a sleepless night, but a row I am not proud of. What a start to a holiday! I guess it wasn't all bad. I recall we visited Anne Frank House. I had been to Bergen-Belsen, where Anne Frank had perished and so found the visit thought-provoking in many ways. At the other end of the scale we visited the 'Sex Museum' at the bottom of Damrak amidst the tackiest part of town. I remember nothing of it, to be honest, so I guess I put it in my mental 'The Dam' box of the underwhelming. It's a box filled with coffee shops pumping out Bob Marley, with posters of Bob smoking a spliff on the walls, and white mostly Brit kids excitedly inhaling their perceived freedom from mum, dad and suburban life. It wasn't long before my friend, Rob, and I hatched a plan to leave the other two and go in search of the real Amsterdam.

And there is life to this city beyond the uneasy tourist trap for smokers, stags and hens that the Red Light District had become. Years after my then girlfriend and I split, I returned with another pal to celebrate our 30th birthdays. He is now a vicar, but I swear we didn't stay at the Christian Youth Hostel. Maybe our own underwhelming visit to 'The Dam' turned him towards God?

I returned again with work during a very short stint at a hotel booking company in 2006. My colleague and I whizzed round around 20 or 30 hotels in two days, from five star opulence to rickety hostels with steep stairs and only one exit, something that alarmed me, particularly considering the state of many young guests at Amsterdam hostels. The true Amsterdam highlight for me on that whirlwind work visit was the Prins Hendrik Hotel at the end of the Damrak, opposite Centraal Station and at the edge of the Red Light District.

'Would you like to see the Chet Baker room?' asked the hotelier, leading us towards Room 210, named after the famous jazz musician.

'Sure. Did Chet Baker stay here?'

'He died here!' replied the hotelier.

Poor Chet stayed at the Prins Hendrik in 1988 and fell from the window of room 210. Reports state that heroin and cocaine were found in his room, but his death appeared to be an accident. As far as unique selling points go, that's pretty quirky. Only in Amsterdam.

You see, I have tried to love Amsterdam. I have given it plenty of chances. And when I finally got round to putting a rail holiday together to the Netherlands, some years later, it was an altogether better experience. I was accompanied by Jack. Looking back on the trips Jack and I did would sound like a list of lads' trips around Europe, if either of us was in the slightest bit laddish (which we aren't). Prague, Budapest, Berlin, Amsterdam, the list of lads' contracting trips goes on. We decided to go the Hull to Rotterdam overnight ferry route, taking this chapter full circle, but this time in cabins. Despite how this chapter began, I really do like the overnight ferries from Hull. There is plenty to do on board to while away the evening and those reclining seats and sticky carpets are a thing of the past.

The trip went swimmingly, visiting quaint Haarlem, home of the Dutch master Frans Hals, and even more quaint Delft, all gabled houses criss-crossed by canals and the place that gave the world Delft pottery. Amongst the hotel visits we visited the local museum, the Prinsenhof, learning that this had been the home of the first William of Orange, leader of the Dutch rebellion against Spanish Habsburg rule. The bullet holes remain in the wall from his assassination in 1584 by Catholic supporter of Philip of Spain, Balthasar Gérard, who was subsequently found, tried and brutally executed for the deed.

If you aren't interested in the tourist trap of the Amsterdam Red Light District (and I'm not), it's not hard to find the real Amsterdam. It is a great city, actually, with so many gorgeous gabled buildings, canals, museums, nightlife and neighbourhoods to be explored, which Jack and I did after our days' work. So much so that I came away, fifth or sixth time of asking, actually liking the city and I will be back.

We hit some rail delay issues on the way back to Rotterdam for the return overnight ferry crossing. The ferry operator transfers passengers from central Rotterdam by coach to Europoort. From the train to that last transfer coach was the fastest this middle-aged man has ever run pulling a case, but once on board we relaxed in the piano bar with a

Hoegaarden as nightcap, knowing we'd wake up the following morning refreshed and ready to go straight into work. 'We must do this again,' we smugly decided. 'What a civilised way to reach the Low Countries or Germany from the north of England.'

Morning came, the long trawl through the Humber Estuary finally brought us to the Port of Hull, with the Zeebrugge ferry already in its dock and our own dock just a couple of hundred metres away. What happened next was inexplicable. Our dock, instead of getting closer, just gradually slipped into the distance, we seemed to be making the same journey back out of the Humber Estuary, back out to a stormy North Sea. Eventually it became clear, that the tide and wind had changed direction, docking had been deemed too dangerous and we had sailed out to sea for our own safety. With little to no wifi signal and a bored passenger public with an extra six hours at sea, the on-board cinema was reopened and Kung Fu Panda 2 would be shown. With no kids on board this midweek crossing and the ship rocking in the high waves. There is a direct Eurostar service to Amsterdam from London now. Just saying.

Chapter 19 - Molli, Roland & Sam

'Is there anything I can bring you from Yorkshire as a thank you?'
Together with a few friends I had set up an official fanclub in
Leeds for Hamburg's FC St Pauli, an eternally underachieving
football club on the pitch but overachieving off it in terms of
community spirit. Sönke, a very active person in the fan scene in
Hamburg itself, had been a great help to us. My work trip would end in
Hamburg with a bit of pleasure, watching a St Pauli match live with
friends and fellow fans from all over the world.

'Some Sam Smiths Organic Chocolate Stout,' was Sönke's reply.

I was working in York, of course, just down the road from Samuel
Smith's Tadcaster brewery, but Sönke's treasured black gold was not
easy to find. Eventually I found a pub with two bottles of the stuff,
snaffled both and packed them into my trusty case, which was well
padded out with the fanclub's huge 'Yorkshire St Pauli' banner that I
would hang behind the goal at the end of the working week.

Flying into Hanover, but overnighting in Rostock threw up two
options. The first was changing in Hamburg on trains and tracks I had
used many times. The second option was more convoluted and
involved changes in unheard of stations in Nowheresville, Lower
Saxony. I think you will have guessed by now that I chose the second
option.

Have you ever had that feeling when you just happen upon
something great? I wish I could say I had planned it. Planning great

holidays by rail was my job, after all. But, well, I have to be honest and it just wasn't planned. My route through rural Lower Saxony and into Mecklenburg Vorpommern, the northernmost of the new states that joined the German Federation from the GDR after reunification, involved a 20 minute of so change in Bad Uelzen. Bad Where?

When I stepped off the train I stepped into another world. If I didn't have to be somewhere else I would have stayed much longer. My first thought was that this unassuming small town station's unique design reminded me of the Hundertwasser House in Vienna, designed by the artist and architect Friedensreich Hundertwasser. If you haven't been, it's a block of flats whose windows have individual shapes and styles, with trees and plants growing out of every crack, bringing architecture back to nature.

It turned out that it was indeed the work of Hundertwasser, who chose this backwater town on a railway junction to design an 'environmentally culturally oriented' station. Bad Uelzen's façade looked to me like a Moorish palace crossed with a surrealist flourish of Salvador Dali-type craziness. I took a quick wander into the town to check that the rest of the place wasn't equally mad. I soon headed back. It was just the station. And what a station! The ticket hall and stairwell into the subterranean part of the building are gems, as are the loos. Yes, the loos! Now, I'm not generally a fan of railway station bogs, but I'd spend a penny in Bad Uelzen's work-of-art Gents any day of the week.

Rostock, late Sunday evening, and all was quiet. I remembered to remove my FC St Pauli cap before arriving into the home city of my team's arch rival, FC Hansa Rostock, stared thirstily at the two bottles of Sam Smith's Organic Chocolate Stout in my case, but left them in situ for Sönke. An early night was required as tomorrow would be a busy day.

Rivalry aside, Rostock is a pleasant enough old Hanseatic city and port, with the added attraction of seaside Warnemünde a hop, skip and a jump away by very efficient public transport. But after a morning of hotel visits, it was a different coastline I was looking for, reached in romance and nostalgia on the Mecklenburgische Bäderbahn, or "Molli" as she is better known to the outside world.

This has to be one of my favourite train journeys. It is such a special little section of track. From the small town station at Bad Doberan, just west of Rostock, Molli steams steadily through the middle of a shopping street, past the little hotel, the bakery and the cafés, past mothers pushing prams and the town's senior folk having a natter on the pavement. It's an everyday occurrence here to smell the soot and hear the whistle of a Class 99 steam locomotive as you sip your coffee and peruse the local newspaper in the Café Zikke.

A stretch of narrow gauge railway was opened here in 1886 between Bad Doberan and the upmarket resort of Heiligendamm, before being extended in 1910 all the way to Kühlungsborn, the biggest coastal town in Mecklenburg. It's a very lovely stretch of just over 15km of track. After the initial charm of trundling along the Goethestrasse shopping street, the landscape opens out into fields, with Molli puffing her way along an alluring avenue of linden trees on her way towards the pleasures of the beach. Heiligenbad is first up, the first German seaside resort and known as 'the White Town on the Sea', with a lovely pier, beautiful buildings and high-end hotels. With limited time I stayed on until Kühlungsborn, although this in itself threw up a quandary. There are three stations. Ost services the beach resort, Mitte the town and shops, whilst West at the line's terminus houses the railway's museum. I chose Ost, taking the steps our customers would take, wandering down past the white painted villas, cafés and hotels to the sea, where I found Kühlungsborn's 240 metre long pier and a six kilometre stretch of sand. These resorts have a nostalgic charm, but without the faded glory of the British seaside. On a crisp but sunny early March day it was a lovely place to be.

Alas, it was already early afternoon and I had a hire car to pick up. From Bergen on the island of Rügen. Some 170km away. Molli meandered her way back to Bad Doberan in time for me to join the main network and, with a change in Rostock, just under two hours later I was crossing over the bridge from the UNESCO World Heritage and Hanseatic city of Stralsund on the German mainland onto the holiday island of Rügen and Bergen, the main working town of the island.

The beaches, the resplendent white villas, the vast flat plains of Pomerania, you tend to forget that you are in what was Soviet-controlled East Germany. In fact, you can't get much farther east that Rügen in today's Germany. Once outside Bergen station I stumbled upon a curio, a memorial column with a red star emblazoned on the front, surrounded by a number of small, flat gravestones. It turned out to be the resting place of 53 of the Red Army's fallen soldiers. Yes, this is definitely the East.

My 24 hour car hire collected, I drove out of Bergen through a country idyll, detouring along the island section of the 'German Avenue Road', a tourist route linking tree-lined avenues from Rügen in the Northeast to Lake Constance on the Swiss border. Having sampled my bit of Germany's longest tourist route, I arrived at my hotel amidst the greenery of the island's flat northern coast, a short walk from a deserted beach (it was winter...and evening) surrounded by reed beds, birdlife and nature. 'What an unspoilt part of Europe,' I thought, cradling the nightcap treat I'd afforded myself after such a long day's travelling, a glass of draught Störtebeker, brewed nearby in Stralsund. Störtebeker was a semi-fictitious German pirate and the glass had a beautifully crafted ship's funnel shape to it. In a moment of instinctive piracy the glass somehow ended up in my case with Sönke's Sam Smith's Organic Chocolate Stout.

The following day was spent driving around Rügen on the trail of the 'Racing Roland', the cute nickname for the Rügensche Bäderbahn, a narrow-gauge railway connecting several beauty spots on the island. I was trying to understand how best to deal with a group's expectations in terms of experience of the steam trains, as well as the accessibility of the resorts from the stations. The groups would have hop-on, hop-off tickets but I wanted to make sure they didn't hop off somewhere they'd be stranded. Some of the stations might be too far from the sea or inaccessible for people with walking difficulties, so I drove from the railway's start point in Putbus to Binz, Sellin and its terminus in Göhren.

If you haven't been to Rügen the names won't mean much. Binz, the largest resort on the island, is gorgeous but just too far away to walk from the steam train station. Then there's Sellin, with its Ost and West stations, glistening white villas and the most incredible seaside pier I have ever seen. But way too far to walk from the steam train stations.

Pleasant if less spectacular Göhren was manageable on foot, so got the nod. All the while, Racing Roland himself criss-crossed my path as I drove, tooting smugly at me as I waited patiently at level crossings, stuck in a hire car and unable to join the fun.

On my way back to drop off the car off in Bergen I took a slight detour. Prora was the concept of 'Kraft durch Freude' or 'Strength through Joy', the world's largest tour operator in the 1930s. Sounds ominous? It doesn't quite have the same ring to it as Thomas Cook or Wallace Arnold, I think you would agree. Well, yes, that's because Prora was built by the Nazis before World War II as a colossal holiday resort. It was a series of concrete blocks running alongside the beach stretching for almost three miles without break, a sort of huge holiday factory for the masses to enjoy a break from their own factories gearing up for world domination. You can picture the propaganda for Prora, the blond, bronzed, sunkissed Aryan idyll of the family unit, relaxing by the sea amidst thousands of other identikit blond, bronzed, sunkissed Aryan family units.

The holiday resort was never realised and a smaller than original Prora lay underused for decades, yet still measuring almost two miles in length. A two mile long hotel, for heaven's sake! Wandering around a disused part of the site I got caught short. It's an age thing, I guess. Whilst I'm not usually one for urinating in public places, or even writing about urinating in general actually, I did somehow gain a perverse pleasure from peeing up the wall of Hitler's Grand Hotel.

Car deposited in Bergen, a quick change in Stralsund, and the RE (Regional Express) train took me southwards through sleepy northeastern Germany to the capital for the ITB, the world's biggest travel trade fair. Berlin is covered elsewhere, so let's just say I booked my usual Berlin accommodation for ITB, a single en-suite room in a cheap youth hostel on the Ringbahn, Berlin's orbital train route. Whilst basic, it has a direct connection to the fair and is just five minutes by train from Prenzlauer Berg in one direction and Friedrichshain in the other, two great places to chill out of an evening after a day running from stand to stand. I had, however, taken the risk of booking my then boss into the same abode.

'Heyyyyy…..we're from facking Polaaaaand!!'

East Berlin was already in mid-evening darkness as I approached the hostel from the station. A group of Polish lads were hanging out of a second floor window, goading another group of lads down below in the car park.

'Well fack youuuuuu!! We're from facking Denmaaaaark!!' screamed the boys from below, beating their little Danish chests.

'Fack meeeeee,' I thought, 'the boss is NOT going to like this place!'

It took some time before he finally recovered from the youth hostel experience. As for me, settled into my box room I admit that I opened my case, spotted the sexy funnelled Störtebeker glass and the two bottles of Sam Smith's Organic Chocolate Stout that I had already dragged around a few hundred miles of northern Germany for Sönke. And I drank one of them. A little bit too sweet for my palate. Sorry Sönke.

Friday arrived and one of Deutsche Bahn's speedy, comfortable and efficient ICE (Inter City Express) trains shuttled me to Hamburg in time for the game. A contact at Maritim Hotels had arranged a room for me at their hotel opposite the main station, so I could just drop my bag and head for St Pauli. But I couldn't just drop my bag.

Checking in, the penny dropped when they handed me my room key. The key fob had the badge of FC St Pauli on it. I put the key in the room door and it chimed, 'bonggg, bonggg,' to the opening bars of 'Hell's Bells' by ACDC, the St Pauli team's entrance music. Once inside there was a bed with a St Pauli duvet cover, St Pauli pillows and a huge St Pauli emblem on the wall above it. The loo (yes, more toilets! Is this the toilet chapter?!) had St Pauli tiles, the walls were adorned with St Pauli memorabilia. I felt like a little boy who had just found the last Panini sticker to complete the full set. In St Pauli itself I located Sönke and delivered the remaining bottle of Sam Smith's Organic Chocolate Stout. St Pauli delivered three points. I jumped, bounced and sang with my friends on the terraces, then, much to the annoyance of guests in the neighbouring rooms, spent the night opening and closing my door to hear more of ACDC. Hell's bells!

Chapter 20 - The Italian Job

I love Italy. The effortless style of the people, the artistic masterpiece cities, the perfection of the Italian Lakes, the food and, most of all, the inherent hospitable nature of Italians. As a destination Italy always throws up challenges though. It isn't the easiest to deal with in terms of planning holidays, so you do have to take the rough with the smooth sometimes. Having watched colleagues tear their hair out trying to deal with Italian hoteliers and suppliers, wondering what the hell they talked about during those emotionally charged hour long phone conversations in a language I barely understood. Why all the fuss? I didn't have to endure hours of tears, arguments and stress with my logical, business-like northern European hoteliers. Finally, though, the attractive, popular, stylish yet troublesome problem child destination, Italy, was moved to my team and I would be destined to spend lots of time there.

Let us start this chapter at one of the Milan airports. I forget which. The first destination would be an Italian lake. I've done them all, mostly reached from Milan, but also Bergamo, Verona, Treviso or Venice. Please take your pick as it could be any of those. I never forget railway stations, but soulless airports don't feature in my limited brainspace.

This chapter isn't about Lake Garda, which is probably the easiest of the Italian lakes for me. There are loads and loads of hotels around the lake and I have personal friends there who have looked after my groups for the last twenty years, irrespective of which company I was working for. It is a lake full of contrasts. The coach operators prefer the northern part of the lake, accessed over the Brenner Pass, with resorts like Riva del Garda, Torbole sul Garda and honeypot Malcesine basking by the lake yet backed by brooding pre-alpine mountains. The rail tour operators prefer the south, simply due to connections, with railway stations at Peschiera and Desenzano accessed via high-speed routes through France. Though flat by contrast and with an almost Mediterranean resort feel, the proximity of the south's own honeypot, Sirmione, helps tourism here massively.

Occupying a slender spit on the southern shores of the lake, like a little upside down uvula in Lake Garda's thriving throat, Sirmione seemingly helps the southern lakeside towns keep the waves under control. You enter through a gate in the medieval wall of the 13th century Scagilero castle, both sides of the hire care virtually touching the stonework, perspiring, expecting to hear an ominous scraping metallic sound at any moment, before eventually manoeuvring through narrow streets thronged with carefree crowds. It is a stunning spot, a lovely place to go wandering around the walls and beyond, or to relax with a gelato and enjoy la bella vita.

There is one way in and one way out of Sirmione, across that bridge and through the castle gate. A traffic light system helps direct the traffic, with permits required to bring a car onto the tip of the peninsula. The red light can be easily missed when desperately trying not to run over carefree, gelato-licking tourists or scrape the sides of your hire car on ancient stonework. Having negotiated my way out of the Old Town and with another hotel appointment looming, I suddenly found I had a whole different negotiation to consider. A middle-aged policewoman flagged me down and took me into her office, probably rubbing her hands at the sight of the latest lummox to have lost sight of the red light. Thankfully my approximation of the Hugh Grant character worked. You know the one, it's his only character, after all; the foppish, bashful, vaguely charming yet hapless Englishman. My wife will be reading this in fits of laughter, no doubt, but the Carabinieri put the charge in the bin. I departed with a stern telling off but no fine.

The east of the lake is punctuated with great resorts, like Garda itself and Bardolino, with a wonderful wine region as a backdrop. The west of the lake is a little less accessible and a little more mysterious, but Gardone Riviera has to be one of the lake's loveliest locations and I'll never forget sitting patiently in the lounge of the Savoy Palace Hotel with my obligatory caffè waiting for the Sales Manager to show me around. An older German couple arrived at the reception desk to check in, cases in tow, clearly flustered from the hours belting through Austria and across the Brenner in their BMW to 'Gardasee', where German is second language due to the number of tourists making that same simple trip from the German speaking countries. The receptionist tapped their name into his machine, but there appeared to be no booking. A verbal exchange happened, with receptionist frantically trying to find their reservation, making phone calls to management, with the tension that things could get heated at any point with the increasingly belligerent couple berating the hotel, Italy and its non-Germanic disorganised chaos. Now rumbling through their suitcases, eventually the couple found their paper reservation and indignantly presented it to the poor receptionist.

'Your booking is for the Savoy Palace in Riva del Garda. This is the Savoy Palace in Gardone Riviera.'

The couple, stopped dead in their tracks and now with nobody else to blame, not the receptionist, nor the hotel's inefficient reservations system, nor Italy itself, asked how far away their Savoy Palace would be?

'About 50 kilometres. You probably drove past it an hour ago.'

When the couple had disappeared back to their BMW to sheepishly retrace their tracks northwards, no doubt having a domestic as they drove around the very beautiful and relatively undeveloped northwestern shore of Lake Garda, we all had a good chuckle at their expense. It's called Schadenfreude in German, I believe.

Across the road is a tourist site that conjures up a whole pandora's box of emotions in different people, from curiosity to pilgrimage to offence and horror. 'Il Vittoriale degli italiani', a monument to the victories of the Italians, is the folly of Gabriele d'Annunzio, with amphitheatre, mausoleum and bizarrely even a section of the Puglia ship jutting out from the hillside, pointing in the direction of the Adriatic in anticipation of reconquering lost neighbouring territories. D'Annunzio is a controversial figure. A writer, poet, politician and an aristocrat with the title Prince of Montenevoso, he became a bit of a

First World War hero in the fascist Italy of the 1920s and 30s. The swashbuckling image is of the pilot who flew an air raid over Vienna in 1918 to drop leaflets he had written imploring the Viennese to revolt against their Prussian masters. Though never officially a fascist, his legacy for many lies more in his influence on Mussolini and the Italian fascist movement.

If that's not thought-provoking enough, the next village is Salò. During the latter part of World War II, when Mussolini's grip on power was fading, his second fascist republic was based in the unassuming and undeniably otherwise very pleasant lakeside town of Salò between 1943 and 1945. The Nazi-backed puppet state was even known as the Republic of Salò.

Leaving the west of the lake and its dodgy history behind, the great thing about basing yourself in Desenzano on the gently lapping southern shore, apart from the boat access to the other resorts, is that Venice is just a direct train ride away and you arrive right at the centre at Santa Lucia station, with the canal directly in front of you. But I seem to have forgotten that this chapter is not about Lake Garda. Nor is it about Lake Maggiore, when in truth it should be. You see, Maggiore is the best Italian Lake for a rail holiday. When the line from Milan hits the lake on the right hand side you are rewarded with the absolutely stunning scenery of the Borromean Islands. From swish resorts aware of their past glories, such as Stresa, you can sail to the islands, Isola Bella, Isola Madre and Isola dei Pescatori. What's more, if you take the train farther north to the junction town of Domodossola, a line that would eventually continue on the Simplon route through the Alps into Switzerland, you can switch onto the Centovalli Railway, a tourist route through 'a hundred valleys' to Locarno in Ticino, the Italian-speaking part of Switzerland and the Swiss arm of Lake Maggiore. A boat then brings you back across the lake and the international boundary to Stresa, completing one of the best day trips you will ever experience.

But this trip didn't begin on Lake Maggiore either. Nor did it encompass Lake Lugano, which to be fair is mostly in Switzerland and has its own assortment of rail fun on the Swiss side in the twin mountain funiculars, Monte Bre and the San Salvatore, like two bookends with Lugano's hotels occupying the shelves like a proud set of romantic novels. No, my colleague picked me up from Como station in her hire car, flustered by driving in Italy and without a sat nav. It was late evening, she was late, having had many failed attempts to find the railway station, but we finally made it to Cernobbio for the first night.

Como, at first sight from my previous visit, had become my favourite Italian lake. It is just so perfectly framed and you could imagine why George Clooney, amongst others, preferred to live there. Bellagio, on a spit where the lake splits into two strands, is a beauty spot that takes some beating. The previous trip had been to solve a problem. Our hotel, the only one on the lake to offer all-inclusive, had been very poorly received. It did not have enough public space to accommodate the number of people staying there and the bar was in a dingy cellar. Meal times were a bunfight of a buffet, serving the kind of approximation of 'Italian' food my mum would have conjured up in the 1980s. In other words, spaghetti, mince and tomato sauce with not a herb or spice in sight. Our customers hated it, the company wouldn't drop it as it was a big seller, so to tick the bosses' boxes I had to drive around the lake visiting every hotel, inevitably reporting back that no other hotel would offer all-inclusive at low prices. The only option was to try to polish the rough diamond as best I could. I had managed to get the hotelier to give our groups a private room for dinner, lessening the stress of pitched battles over garlic bread, but the complaints had continued.

So here I was again, tasked with taking my colleague around the lake this time, visiting those same hotels, drawing the inevitable same conclusion, in order that this time the boss's boss could tick the right boxes for his boss. I enjoyed the ferry across to Bellagio and I enjoyed quaint Varenna too on the right bank. I had a quiet chuckle as well at my colleague struggling to function without a sat nav whilst driving around a bloody great big lake, where, let's face it, you have a big body of water either to the left or the right to help you navigate. It just felt like a waste of a time, travel for the sake of it.

My colleague dropped me back in Como, then headed home, whereas I embarked on the next stage of the trip. I made my way to Milano Centrale, another Italian curio from a different era. It's a bombastic building, there is no question. No doubt it ranks highly on many lists of iconic railway stations, those cathedrals of the railways, but, opened in 1931 under Mussolini, who wanted the pompous grand design to reflect Italy's fascist state power, I find I cannot worship at this particular cathedral, preferring to get in and out as quickly as possible.

Trenitalia's inter-city services are fast, comfortable, efficient and affordable. It is possible to connect Milano Centrale with Firenze Santa Maria Novella station in around two hours with a couple of stops, one of which will be Bologna. I would meet another of my team, Meg, at the Florence hotel. We'd spend one night in the Renaissance masterpiece city, with a few hotel visits and a meal at a restaurant serving local Florentine and Tuscan specialities. Meg, an Italian speaker with a passion for cheese, had put together a mouth-watering tour with gastronomy as the theme.

I don't recall much of the hotel rooms we were shown, but, we were shown pools on rooftops and, wow, the views over the city were simply untouchable, with the iconic Duomo dominating the skyline. The restaurant featured in the gastronomic tour really wanted to impress too, the owner and the chef continually arriving at our table with extra courses of delicious local specialities. There was no spag bol here. We had asked to eat the same three courses our groups would enjoy, yet we were completely stuffed before the first of those courses arrived!

Florence was the starter in our two course Tuscan taster trip. The main course would be Montecatini Terme, a small Tuscan spa town with lots of affordable hotels, around an hour away from Florence on a pleasant regional train journey. Our new Tuscany tour based there was full, ten or twelve departures, and the first couple had returned with complaints about the meals at our 4* grand hotel, sourced by a former colleague. We had around 24 hours in Montecatini, staying at said hotel, to have a look around, visit a small number of alternative future possibilities and to try to get underneath the issues with the food with the hotel staff.

The Sales Manager arrived and took us up the hotel's open staircase towards the bedrooms, which were located on several floors. After the show round we were due to discuss the complaints and make diplomatic but firm suggestions on how to improve feedback from guests. Between the staircase and the very first room we were shown I mumbled into Meg's ear, 'Let's make our excurses and get out of here as quickly as we can!'

When we had run around our truncated tour of the hotel, politely refusing a meeting or even a coffee with the Sales Manager, we made it outside. When Meg asked what was wrong, I explained. The hotel had one exit from its several storeys, that main staircase. It had no fire doors. It had no smoke alarms. Forget about food; that hotel was an inferno waiting to happen! We sprinted to the tourist office, picked up a list of hotels and divided twenty of them between us. We had ten or twelve groups to relocate and just 24 hours in which to do it.

That was my experience of Montecatini Terme, looking at bedroom ceilings for smoke alarms, checking corridors for fire doors and emergency exits. In amongst the panic and fluster of flitting from hotel to hotel, we found somewhere that would fit the bill, then raced to our train. A short regional train ride took us back to Florence, where we rejoined Italy's mainline to Rome Termini, a fast, comfortable service that takes about 1 ½ hours. With an evening arrival we managed to check a few Rome hotels too. The following day I would leave Meg there to visit more options, so my late evening was spent sightseeing alone. You never know when you will return to a place and so I find I need to make use of every spare minute. Does anyone else do this? I will concede that it is slightly bonkers to sightsee around the Vatican City at midnight with a flight to catch early the following morning, but it is in my blood. Travel, I mean, not Catholicism! I didn't manage to see the Pope, but, hey, I think I will cope.

Chapter 21 - A load of Blarney

R ewind! Rewind back to the depths of time. Back to last century, in fact, for that's when I first clapped eyes on the Emerald Isle on what was also my first holiday by rail.

I wonder to myself occasionally how it came about that I would make a career (some would say a life, it is that important to me) out of rail holidays. I hark back to this particular holiday or maybe that one, where I hopped on a train to go sightseeing, not really considering the mode of transport. Truthfully though, a trip to Ireland in the mid-90s is where it really started.

We set out after work from Manchester Piccadilly, about ten of us, armed with three or four tents and a through ticket that packaged a rail return to Holyhead with ferry crossings to Dublin. Or was it Dun Laoghaire? I honestly can't remember. The outbound journey was a blur in which none of us slept. We were taking the night ferry, hoping that a swift Guinness would induce a sleepiness, crawling into a corner of the boat for a kip, waking up to the fair old mountain dew of the Old Country the following misty morn. That was the romantic notion from a twenty-something weekend backpacker, as I was back then. It wasn't to be.

You will discover the delights of the North Wales Coast line later in this book, hopefully sharing with me the sea, the slate hills and a mysterious corner of Britain with its own language. As the train darts along the shore it's ocean views, Snowdon's peaks in the distance,

Anglesey popping into view, the Menai Straits bridges, Lanfairpwllgwyngyllgogerychwrndrobllllantysiliogogogoch, then Holyhead, the end of the line. Next stop Ireland.

In my early days in the travel industry, the days before the internet, to conjure up holiday ideas we had to request brochures from tourist boards, which would list attractions and their phone numbers. I remember one from the North Wales Tourist Board that somehow didn't do its wonderful product anything like the justice it deserved. Castles, beaches, mountains, railways of all types and charming resorts like Llandudno, this should be easy work, surely, for any marketeer worth their salt. North Wales has more than enough to fill the pages of any prospectus, but my overriding memory of this particular one from the late 90s is of an advertisement for a 'sheep theatre'. Yes, there was a picture of a sheep on a stage. This thing existed. Briefly, at any rate, as I cannot for the life of me find any mention of it being a real thing, though I am absolutely positive I didn't dream it up. Maybe it's a crazy Welsh thing. After all, there is also the Baked Bean Museum of Excellence in Aberavon near Port Talbot, run by a chap who identifies himself as Mr Beany!

Oh, and the other memory of that particular North Wales Tourism brochure was that their 'excursion suggestions' included a trip Ireland. In other words, we aren't very confident in our ability to entertain you with our Sheep Theatre, so perhaps you would like to bog off to another country for the day instead!

I digress. No, it wasn't to be, the old sleeping on the boat thing. What we hadn't counted on was that Celtic Football Club was playing a friendly match against the Republic of Ireland national side that weekend at Dublin's Lansdowne Road in a testimonial game for Ireland's manager and former Celtic player, Mick McCarthy. The overnight ferry was full of Celtic fans hell-bent on drinking the bar dry, the ferry was rocking and, oh boy, was it raucous!

The sun was rising as we approached Dublin (or Dun Laoghaire – I still don't remember), with the Wicklow Mountains in the distance beyond. There was something mystical about the experience for me, a kind of homecoming of sorts due to my ancestry, or maybe it was the lack of sleep. Dublin was not our final destination, though. I groggily welcomed a greasy spoon breakfast, then a bleary-eyed beer in a bar somewhere, god knows where, before we landed at Heuston Station for the Inter City service across Ireland to the Republic's second city, Cork.

The organisation of this trip was nothing to do with me, you will be shocked and surprised to discover. I was going with the flow with a bunch of friends for a few days. In Cork we would be camping on a campsite near the airport. 'Why didn't you just fly there from Manchester?' you will reasonably be asking now. Well, it all sounds so simple these days, doesn't it? But this was before Ryanair and the budget airline boom. And besides, why fly when you can take a pretty nice train journey across Ireland's green underbelly in the June sunshine?

Heuston Station did not feel much different to home until my eyes spied the first sign of cultural difference on a fellow passenger, a lanky bloke with long wavy black hair, an eye-patch and a Bobby Sands tee-shirt. The train was comfortable and not crowded. The scenery was as you'd expect of the Emerald Isle, green, peaceful and rural. The stations I can still recall, although one or two are now no longer served by the Cork Inter City route. Kildare, Portarlington, Portlaoise, Thurles, Limerick Junction, Mallow and finally Cork Kent Station. Though the scenery looked familiar between these two islands connected by a turbulent history, the pristine, white painted houses and the sheer space around them were more reminiscent to my mind of continental Europe. Ireland was proudly European, even then. From Cork a taxi whisked us off to our camping grounds in the countryside on the edge of the city.

That taxi driver almost became a friend by the end of those few days. It was our mode of transport of choice. Well, there wasn't really a choice from our campsite. Kinsale on the coast was memorable for its brightly painted houses, its coves and beaches, upmarket pubs, and the James and Charles Forts across the bay. It has since become a foodie destination with a Michelin starred restaurant and several culinary events. Blarney, well that's another story. After our taxi driver pal dropped us off we climbed the steps of Blarney Castle to queue behind the Americans to kiss the Blarney Stone in the hope of gaining the gift of the gab. Finally, having waited what seemed like an age behind complaining tourists from across the Pond, my turn arrived. If you haven't had the pleasure, you sit on the edge of the rampart and a guy holds you whilst you bend backwards over a grate that stops you falling headfirst to your ineloquent death. The Blarney Stone is built into the battlements at an awkward angle. Awkward for me anyway as I have, let's say, a larger than average nose. Try as a might to pucker up to Pierre, I just couldn't make my lips reach the stone. So a shy and quiet Yorkshire lad I remain.

Having queued for an hour, having bent precariously over a castle wall, having air-kissed a bit of rock, the day was otherwise perfect. We bought a football from the shop, plus a crate of beer, then goofed around in the sunshine in Blarney's Square, a beautiful green space in the village centre. We had pizza, goofed around some more, before retiring to the pub as darkness fell. Taxi!!!

Cork itself was a pleasant place to be in early summer. With a population significantly smaller than my hometown, it had so much more going on both socially and culturally. One evening we went to the theatre to see a local play, a tragi-comedy. Or maybe it was just a comedy, I am still not sure. It was in the pleasing-to-the-ear but hard to decipher local Cork twang, which has an intonation of its own. The tragedy was that the rest of the audience was in hysterics with laughter, such was the quality of the quips, yet we were seconds behind with every joke, translation cogs whirring wildly. That's assuming we got the jokes at all.

Despite the culture, the music, the social life, dare I say it the craic, there was still a pace of life in Ireland's second city that I admired and coveted. As he drove us over the River Lee one day our taxi driver came to a halt. Another taxi coming the opposite way did exactly the same. The two drivers wound down their windows and, with passengers in the back, passing the time of day as if it were break time in the taxi driver mess room.

'Did you hear about that there Roy Keane?'

'No, what's the feckin eejit done now?'

Cork's finest footballer had failed to report for Mick McCarthy's testimonial game against Celtic that weekend, or indeed the Republic of Ireland training, having gone on holiday instead to Italy. McCarthy would subsequently strip Keane of the Republic captaincy and leave him out of the national team for six matches. It was big news in Cork. I think he had switched off the meter, maybe he hadn't, but somehow we didn't care anyway as we listened on to the endearing chat. What was the hurry anyway? Arriving back into a manically busy Manchester Piccadilly in rush hour at the end of our return journey home, I would have given anything to be back in that cab, back in Ireland's easy-paced southwest.

Chapter 22 - Dublin Up

I did get back to Dublin, a city that conjures up fond memories. From that first glimpse from the deck of the night ferry, having escaped the Celtic shenanigans in the bar, to the next and subsequent visits back to a country my ancestors left a century earlier. My next trip was not work either. It was my honeymoon, the aftermath of a winter wedding spent touring my new wife's home country in her sporty company car. We began in Dublin's genteel seaside south, with a sea view of Killiney Bay, beach walks and the DART (Dublin Area Rapid Transit) station across the way. The brochures likened the bay to the Bay of Naples and, in the February sea fret, if you squinted hard enough you could just about see Sorrento in the distance. Or was that Bray?

Actually, it was nothing like that. The weather was fine, we walked up to Killiney Hill and Dalkey, quite a posh part of the Dublin suburbs that boasted houses owned by Bono and Enya. We went for beach walks, had tea in the beautifully bourgeois Bewley's, glimpsed the ancient Book of Kells at Trinity College and toured the city like two travel-mad travel people would. I even took Maeve to Kilmainham, the gaol that in its time housed a who's who of future Irish politics and society.

'You got married, Maeve! Congratulations! Where did your new husband take you on honeymoon?'

'To a prison.'

She is a lucky lass!

On a serious note, Kilmainham I would recommend to anyone with an interest in Irish history, particularly the events surrounding the Easter Rising. Prominent Republican leaders such as Robert Emmet, Charles Stewart Parnell, Patrick Pearse, James Connolly and Joseph Plunkett were detained here and there are certainly a few railway stations in Ireland named after those former inmates of that gaol. Add into the mix Constance Markievicz, the suffragette and first woman elected to the Westminster parliament, and Éamon de Valera, the Republic's first Taoiseach or Prime Minister no less. The poignant end to the visit is the yard in which the leaders of the 1916 Easter Rising were executed, which is thought-provoking and heart-wrenching to say the very least.

We are still together, Maeve and I, so the following week touring the wild romantic Atlantic coastline of Connemara and then her ancestral home of Athlone at the very centre of Ireland must have made up for the prison faux pas. I don't recall much of Athlone save the bar at the end of her mam's old street, which claims the title of Ireland's oldest public house, though I would imagine there are a few pubs dotted around the 'Old Country' with a similar claim.

That trip was pure pleasure, blissful wintry days with the love of my life, a person who for years afterwards held the fort back home whilst I raced around making holidays. Back to work then, back to early autumn 2013. With a UK programme now booming, my idea was to replicate that boom with our near neighbour, a destination with just one tour in the company's brochure.

On this particular occasion I whizzed straight out of Dublin from Heuston Station, named after Seán Heuston, a young railwayman who commanded a nearby post during the Easter Rising and one of the men executed at Kilmainham in 1916. Until 1966 the station was called Kingsbridge after the nearby bridge over the Liffey, but it was renamed to commemorate the 50th anniversary of those fateful Easter days. Routes travelling southwest from Dublin depart Heuston and my destination would be Waterford.

This is a charming rural route, cutting through a verdant fertile part of Ireland, such as counties Carlow and Kilkenny. Kilkenny town itself is worth a stop, which is exactly what I did, at MacDonagh Station (renamed in 1966 after Thomas MacDonagh, poet, playwright and political leader executed at, you guessed it, Kilmainham in 1916). There's a castle, a cathedral with an unusual round tower, quaint medieval streets and the Smithwick's Experience for those with a thirst for ale.

Waterford Plunkett Station is the end of the line. Named after Joseph Plunkett (I don't need to tell you the rest, surely!), it sits across the River Suir from the main town itself, whose biggest attraction is Waterford Crystal. It is possible to book a tour to watch the skilled craftsmen and women producing crystal sold the world over. I have done the tour and thoroughly enjoyed it. For railway buffs, the nearby Waterford and Suir Valley Railway is one of Ireland's few heritage railways, a charming 40-minute ride in partially open carriages along the valley of the River Suir with views of Mount Congreve Gardens. The carriages are pulled by a restored Simplex Locomotive, which had an arduous working life in the peat industry in the North of England and Scotland. They are lovely people too, so I would urge you to pay them a visit.

At New Ross, County Wexford, they make the most of their Kennedy connections. For starters there is the Kennedy Homestead, then the JFK Arboretum, the Kennedy Hotel, the Rose Fitzgerald Kennedy Bridge, Kennedy College, hell there's even a statue of himself on the quayside. New Ross was a port, but fell into decline as ships got too big to dock there. Its tourist attractions include the Ros Tapestry, depicting Celtic life. Then there's the Dunbrody Famine Ship on the quayside near the statue of JFK, a replica of the type of vessel that the Kennedys would have crammed onto in the 1840s, fleeing the potato famine for a new life across the Atlantic. These were known as 'coffin ships', yet their passengers were fleeing a humanitarian disaster as absurd as it was deadly. A million people perished in Ireland due to starvation or disease brought on by the loss of their crop, yet they were surrounded by a fertile land that did not belong to them and largely ignored by Westminster. This a sobering place in which to reflect on your own history.

I was picked up from New Ross by Anton and driven to Enniscorthy to spend a night in his hotel, a thriving business in the heart of the

Wexford town. Enniscorthy is a pleasant place to stay, with a Norman castle just across the river and I had arranged a guide to take me to Vinegar Hill. In 1798 United Irishmen rebels, charged with the revolutionary fervour sprouting up across the world, rounded on the Wexford town defended by a small battalion of 300, with the support of local Protestants. The United Irish forces were merciless in taking Enniscorthy, with 100 slain, both from the garrison and civilian population. Houses were set alight. The United Irishmen grouped in their thousands at the Vinegar Hill encampment, controlling County Wexford for a month before their own defeat to the Crown's forces, themselves by that stage vastly superior in number and arms, and who issued a brutal retribution of their own on any rebels that couldn't escape.

What great hosts I had in Enniscorthy though and what a smashing little business they have in the heart of town. After eating local produce in the restaurant we moved through to their lively bar, with a local band playing the traditional Irish music that I love. Anton then took me down underneath the hotel and the street through a tunnel to the secret subterranean door of a nightclub across the road. The club also belonged to his business and, despite this being Sunday night, it was rocking with what I assumed were local farmers letting down their hair.

Bidding farewell to Enniscorthy I caught the train back to Dublin, allowing me to experience most of the Wexford to Dublin route, which includes a stretch that many would consider the most scenic in the Republic.

Travelling northwards make sure you sit on the right-hand side of the train for the panoramic coastal views as the track hugs the cliffside between the seaside towns of Greystones and Bray, then opens out into the vast expanses of Killiney Bay (Ireland's 'Bay of Naples' remember!). Look behind you for the Wicklow Mountains in the distance as the Irish Sea laps onto the seaside shore at Killiney itself. Whilst the coast then disappears momentarily, it appears again with yachts bobbing in the harbour at Dun Laoghaire, the birthplace and childhood home of Bob Geldof. The train then moves through the well-to-do southern suburbs of Dublin, passes Lansdowne Road, home of Irish rugby, before allowing you the choice of Pearse or Connolly stations, for those collecting stations named after the 1916 Easter Rising leaders, or Tara Street if you would rather be dropped right at the heart of Dublin's Liffey-side.

Which is exactly what I did, as I was a little early for my meeting with Irish Rail, set in the old school rabbit warren offices of Connolly Station. I walked across the bridge onto O'Connell Street, passing the statue of O'Connell himself. Outside the GPO Building, significant in its own right within Irish history, stands trade union leader Jim Larkin of the 1913 Dublin Lockout, Ireland's most severe industrial dispute, fought in search of better working conditions for 20,000 strikers.

Fascinated further by its history, its hospitality and its great railway journeys, Ireland would feature more in the next brochure. Little did I know that I wouldn't be around to see those tours depart. Returning home from Ireland I had one day with my family before the next longer trip to the States. The loneliness of constant travel alone was beginning to take its toll on me. More importantly, having never previously felt they had lost out through my regular work away, my wife and daughters started to feel like a one-parent-family. A brutal schedule had left me with two or three days at home in almost a month. Something had to change.

Chapter 23 - Chicago, New Orleans & San Francisco

Travelling long-haul with work needs to have plenty of justification, particularly with a young family at home. Back in the day I would generally get to the USA once a year and this early October trip was to solve a couple of big issues, to test a new rail experience, to check out a couple of hotels for a brand new signature tour idea and to gain as much as possible from every spare minute, as usual.

When I had been given the USA to look after I had initially been underwhelmed, but had grown to love the product, the destination and, yes, the people. This is a people industry, after all, and the Americans do know a thing or two about hospitality. The poisoned chalice I had taken on was a well-worn series, travelling from New York to San Francisco, coast to coast, using AMTRAK sleeper services from Washington DC to Chicago, Chicago to Denver and Flagstaff, Arizona, to Los Angeles. As well as those three nights on the sleeper trains the tour involved no less than nine hotels, fitting around dates set by AMTRAK. 40 groups between April and October, sometimes two or even three per week. Hotels in major cities with major trade fairs and other events needed to fit around the dates pre-agreed with the state rail operator. Nine hotels. Nine cities. Forty times.

The following year's programme was selling well and it threw up some problems. There was a major trade event in Chicago and our hotel partner had refused a couple of prime dates. Then there was the

Americas Cup happening in San Francisco Bay, which was a massive headache, blocking out certain dates across the whole region. A charm offensive was required in both cities to get our groups a bed for the night. Meanwhile, a tour I had produced involving refurbished private historic Pullman sleeper carriages between Chicago and New Orleans was selling well and the opportunity arose to tag along with a scheduled departure.

That's the work blurb out of the way, justifying this trip and this chapter. I clearly feel the need to justify myself, protesting a little too much, I think. The reality was that the week before I had been in Ireland and the week of my return I would be off again. Justifying this amount of travel professionally was easy; justifying it personally and emotionally was trickier. I left from our local station towards York, London and Heathrow for a night at the airport before my flight. As the train pulled away, I could see my young daughters sobbing as they waved from the platform. It is a memory that stayed with me throughout the trip. No, actually it will stay with me forever.

After a transatlantic flight and a night at an airport transit hotel, I headed into Chicago to blitz potential hotels to plug the gaps and to schmooze the Sales Manager of the hotel taking most of our groups into hopefully agreeing to take them all. I had two full days of this and got to know Michigan Avenue, the Magnificent Mile, really well. What struck me was that, unlike some other American cities, Chicago's downtown is a great, vibrant place to be of an evening. Night one was at the landmark Chicago institution, the Allerton Hotel. Night two was at my last resort, the Congress Plaza Hotel, across from Grant Park and with Lake Michigan in sight, but a faded hotel back then with terrible reviews. They could take the problem dates, but at what cost to the company's reputation? In between I must have visited another 20 hotels, not including the Trump, which I blagged my way into just out of curiosity.

The highlight hotel for me was the Intercontinental Magnificent Mile. I had earmarked this hotel for my new tour, basically a higher-end coast to coast experience following exactly the same route and the same cities as the well-trodden one, but this time staying at a talking point hotel in each place. The earmarked New York hotel was the

Waldorf, with a Waldorf Salad included, as well as Eggs Benedict, the two dishes invented in the kitchens of that hotel. The Washington Hotel would be the Willard, where Dr Martin Luther King wrote his 'I have a dream' speech. The Intercontinental Chicago's rooms were nice enough, but the story was in the swimming pool, a junior Olympic-sized effort decorated with exquisite Spanish Majolica tiles. Built in 1929, it is one of the oldest in Chicago, a very beautiful place to be and, historically, it is where future Tarzan actor Johnny Weissmuller trained for the Olympics.

My last stop for the night, the last resort, the Congress Plaza, has an interesting story in its own right. Though I was hoping not to have to use it, due to its faded grandeur, old-fashioned rooms and damning reviews, it would only have been for one night on a three week-long tour. However, I wouldn't have even crossed the threshold of the hotel, had a ten year long strike by cleaning and maintenance staff not ended earlier in the year. Yes, you read that correctly, a ten year strike! It is thought to be the longest hotel strike in history.

130 Congress Plaza workers had walked out of the hotel in June 2003 in response to the hotel's planned wage cuts. The hotel on the south side of the 'Mag Mile' had been opened in 1893 for the World's Columbian Exhibition and had accommodated presidents Grover Cleveland, Teddy Roosevelt and Franklin Roosevelt. But its glory days were long gone.

It was alleged during the conflict that the employees' union had discouraged lucrative customers and events from using the hotel, even sending a 'cow pie valentine' - a heart shaped box filled with dry cow manure - to the offices of The National Center for Agricultural Utilization Research, which was considering hosting a conference at the hotel.

As it turned out, I didn't need to moooove any groups to the Congress Plaza. Job done, I was picked up by the Sales Manager of Pullman Rail Journeys and the man with the coolest name in travel. I had known him for a few years and he is a great guy, Reno Gazzola. Yes, Reno Gazzola. The name conjures up a character from a 1960s or 70s road trip movie, travelling coast to coast on Route 66 in search of the 'American Dream'. In fact, Reno is a charming chap from Boise,

Idaho, who would accompany me on the Pullman train service, sort of coast to coast from Chicago to New Orleans. But first we had a backstory to cover.

George Pullman founded the Pullman Car Company in 1867, manufacturing sleeping cars for the booming railroad industry. Pullman purchased land on the South Side of Chicago, around 15 miles from Downtown, to build a company town bearing his name, providing workers with high standard housing for the period and, of course, charging them rent. What remains is a living Victorian town, kind of a Chicagoan version of Saltaire and designated the Pullman National Monument.

You can take a guided tour of the quaint streets, view the memorabilia in the Visitor Centre and take a look at the historic Hotel Florence, saved from demolition in 1975 and still undergoing painstaking refurbishment by the local authorities. But, for me, the most interesting story was being sidestepped. I had asked to visit the Pullman Porters' Museum. Maybe something had been lost in translation or maybe there was some local politics afoot. I will never know. Disappointed to find it not mentioned in my day's itinerary, I asked whether we could still maybe visit unannounced. Reno made the call, the museum was closed that day and the curator couldn't get there in time to open for us.

What a pity. It's a great story. The vast majority of Pullman porters were African Americans and the porters made up nearly half of the entire workforce, which meant that Pullman was America's largest employer of African Americans. A. Philip Randolph founded the Brotherhood of Sleeping Car Porters in 1925, which developed into a very powerful trade union. In 1937 the Brotherhood negotiated the first ever labour agreement between a company and an African American union, an empowerment that must have been way way ahead of its time. The Pullman Porters' Museum is named after A. Philip Randolph and, well, I guess I can just hope I get back there again one day.

Having driven back into downtown Chicago through some pretty hairy neighbourhoods, then along the lakeshore, Reno took me to meet the president of the modern-day Pullman Rail Journeys company, then through Union Station with the other lucky passengers and onto the awaiting train.

It transpired that Pullman Rail Journeys would hook their restored carriages to the rear of the regular AMTRAK service, travelling overnight from Chicago to New Orleans. Excitedly we walked past the silver AMTRAK cars to the beautifully restored chocolate and orange liveried wagons-lits, reminiscent of the Illinois Central Railroad, a carefully crafted reconstruction of the Pullman experience of the 1930s and 1940s when the name represented gracious service and comfort.

The president had explained that there were around 500 original Pullman rail cars still in existence around the world and that his parent company owned and was restoring around 70, in various states of (dis)repair. Whilst the carriages featured modern amenities such as wifi and air conditioning, the rest of the restoration was historically accurate, including textiles, bedding, china, and even the company uniforms. Aside from the comfortable sleeping cars, the highlight was the sociable round-ended lounge car that had begun its original service in 1917.

I dropped my bag into my compartment, which included a gift bag of toiletries, along with plush towels and a bathrobe, room for storage, an en-suite and a sink. The train host was charming and gracious. The lounge car was a beautiful time capsule in which to watch the world go by, socialising with fellow travellers. The last we saw of AMTRAK was the guards doing their duty as we departed Chicago Union. After that, it was Pullman-style all the way, with hearty, delicious meals conjured up in the tiny galley by a renowned chef, based on original menus from the City of New Orleans service that historically plied this route.

Departing Chicago at around 8pm in the evening, the Pullman guests were as well-oiled as the train as we retired to bed, travelling overnight through Illinois, then cutting into the Deep South. I set my alarm so that I could wake up to the Mississippi and reminisce about my previous time in Memphis. This was a nostalgia trip after all. The rest of the journey through Mississippi into the Louisiana bayou is described in another chapter. Our train managed to get to New Orleans on time for me to bid my wonderful host with a wonderful name farewell, before heading into the bizarre other world of New Orleans on a late summer Saturday night.

Bourbon Street was heaving with revellers. It reminded me of being in a European city with stag and hen parties everywhere, just with live music coming from every bar, party people carrying their beer from bar to bar, and at the top end of the street scantily-clad women dancing on the balconies, trying to catch the eye of potential clients and throwing bead necklaces down at males gawping below. A couple of evening hotel visits later I retired to Decatur Street for my favourite Cajun comfort food, red beans and rice, then relaxed at the familiar carousel bar of the Hotel Monteleone.

The good people at Visit New Orleans had arranged for me to take a boat trip on the bayou to see alligators the following day, like a Louisiana version of the Florida Everglades. The nicest taxi driver I've ever ridden with then transported me to the airport for my flight to San Francisco.

'What?! You flew?! This is supposed to be a book about train travel!'

Trust me, having already been away for nearly a week, there was no way I could have gone from New Orleans to San Francisco by train. Plus, it would have been very convoluted and would have taken me days.

The pleasant Sunday floating with alligators, the even more pleasant Sunday conversation with the cabbie came to a gradual, then unpleasant halt at New Orleans Airport. It was the first time I had flown internally in the States. I checked in using the machine, as requested, and, although I thought it strange that I didn't have a seat number at the point of going to the gate, I thought maybe it was normal. Walking round the gates I soon realised that normal procedure in US aviation entailed overbooking aircraft, as it seemed that several flights were asking for volunteers to stay an extra night in New Orleans.

At my gate the airline staff arrived at the very latest possible moment, then began boarding using row numbers allocated at check-in. Without a row number (or seat on the aircraft), I approached the airline ground crew, who completely blanked my questions. Looking around, it became clear. There were five or six of us, little old British me, a German couple and two or three other foreign nationals. They had bumped the foreigners off the flight. We were going to be given 'an extra night in a New Orleans hotel to enjoy the city some more, plus a flight to San Francisco tomorrow'. It was every man (and woman) for themselves, so, with the aircraft now boarded and steam fizzing from every facial orifice, I made my point forcefully.

'I need to be in San Francisco tomorrow morning to work. I suggest you get me a seat on that plane. Otherwise, you will have to pay for the hotel, for me to fly from here to London tomorrow, then for return flights from London to San Francisco next week.'

'Please wait a moment, sir. We'll ask for a volunteer to give you their seat.'

Before I could counter that I had already paid for a chuffing seat, she was on the walkie-talkie. A minute or so later a guy around my age emerged from the aircraft, fist-pumping and practically jumping for joy at the idea of an extra night in Crazytown, perhaps dreaming of bead throwing scantily clad ladies on Bourbon Street. Impressed by my own unusual bout of assertiveness and grateful to be on the flight, I walked along the cabin to my seat, avoiding the stares of my now delayed and inconvenienced fellow passengers.

'Wow, that's a relief. I nearly didn't make it,' I offered as an introduction to the woman in the adjacent seat, as a grappled with the seatbelt, the rest of the flight impatiently ready for take-off.

'The guy who gave you his seat was my husband!'

Conversation killed, it was a pretty silent flight from that moment on. I was dying to tell her that her hubby had been fist-pumping and jumping for joy at the thought of a night in New Orleans without her, but thought better of it.

Late evening San Francisco. San Francisco Airport, that is. Will in the office had booked my accommodation. Time to take your bow, Will. If you have ever watched the series 'My Name is Earl', this seemed like exactly the same motel featured on that programme, with rooms rentable by the hour. The only catering nearby was a microwaved chilli dog and a can of Bud from the local gas station. I had made it coast to coast and found the 'American Dream'.

Actually, it made me chuckle and I lived to tell the tale. From Will's Motel I took the BART (Bay Area Rapid Transit) the following morning into San Francisco. Whilst the following two days were spent trying to solve a problem, visiting umpteen hotels in Downtown San Francisco, Fishermen's Wharf and even Oakland, San Francisco became the most interesting of American cities for me.

Union Square was busy, but what really struck me was how the city turned from power and potential to abject poverty within two blocks. The kind climate and the liberal local government make San Francisco attractive to the homeless. To watch so many people shuffling around with their worldly goods in a shopping trolley, just a couple of hundred yards from very fancy hotels sums up America in many ways. By contrast, Fishermen's Wharf was very touristy, but enjoyable and how can you not enjoy riding streetcars from hotel to hotel. It's a tough job but someone's gotta do it.

On my last night, mission accomplished to the best of my ability, something unusual happened. Amidst a career of many hundreds of nights spent alone in hotel rooms, eating alone and kicking around towns and cities, on this occasion, by complete fluke, a band was in town that I wanted to see. Suited and booted from my last meeting I very sheepishly wandered into the DNA punk club to purchase a ticket to see a band from Toronto called F**ked Up that evening. The hotel had placed a bottle of Champagne in my room as a thank you for all the business. I necked it, then watched an electrifying set in a small venue by a band I now never miss when they come to Leeds. Champagne and punk rock!

I had one more hotel visit before flying home, in Oakland across the bay at 10am, where I'd also check out Jack London Station, one of the entry points to San Francisco Bay with AMTRAK, with no station in San Francisco itself. But I still hadn't done one pressing tourist thing, Haight Ashbury, epicentre of the 1960s hippy movement. An alarm was set to make sure I was walking the streets towards that famous intersection whilst any normal person would have been in bed.

Immediately before this trip I had been in Ireland for a week. On my return I was in Scotland within a couple of days on another trip. When that period of intense travel was over Mrs C broke it to me that both our daughters had been in tears at school, missing their dad. You could call this a turning point, a eureka moment, that this was not the lifestyle of a family father. You could even call this lifestyle the same name as the band I had seen in San Francisco. A change was overdue. Either a different role within the company or, failing that, a different company entirely.

Chapter 24 - Beers, Tears & Bellyaches

'**P**riorité à droite! Priorité à droite!'
The elderly woman had got out of the car. The car that she had just driven into our hire car. She was waving her arms around and shouting the phrase over and over again. In France they have an ancient law that nobody cares about anymore, apart from this elderly mademoiselle from Armentières. The law that from a minor road you don't have to stop at a junction to a main road. You can just simply carry on, smashing into anything that's in your way. Apparently.

We were on our way from Lille into Belgium. This was the last village in France before the calm of Belgian roads where everyone follows the same rules as the rest of the world about stopping at junctions. With a big dint in the passenger door of our hire car, I pulled it onto the kerb at the behest of the local gendarmerie, whilst Zoë managed to prise herself out of the minor wreckage at her side of the vehicle to dazzle the locals with her French. I'm glad she was there. I was shaken. Whilst I wandered along the side road from which the mademoiselle from Armentières, who hadn't been kissed for forty years, had emerged for her demolition derby, taking pictures of the STOP signs she had ignored, Zoë did the inky pinky parlez vous. Or something.

I was travelling with my team. In the front passenger seat next to the dented door was Zoë, a vivacious francophone, a Pontefract lass with a fascinating family background even more exotic than Ponte Carlo. And I'm not talking Cas Vegas here (Pontefract's neighbouring town, Castleford). Mrs C likes to talk and often refers to the fact that women have 20,000 words to get out of their system every day. As opposed to men, who apparently utter far fewer words, particularly dour Yorkshiremen like this one. Well, let's just say that 20,000 would be a low estimate for Zoë. And that she's a deep and very intelligent woman.

Men apparently only utter around 7,000 words by comparison. Sitting quietly in the back seat was Jack. I haven't mentioned him yet, have I? Well, it's not surprising really is it, as he hasn't said anything yet! With just 7,000 words to get rid of, Jack is cool, quiet, dry-humoured and considerate. The rain now pouring, the leaking door spraying stoical Jack in the back seat, he didn't complain at all. He's loyal, the kind of man you would want standing next to you in the trenches. Which is ironic, as Jack is half-German. And we were on our way to Ypres to plan out a couple of days in the World War I battlefields.

We were trying to cover two days in just one long day, ending with the poignant Last Post Ceremony at the Menin Gate in Ypres, commemorating those who gave their lives in Flanders Fields a century before. Now a couple of hours behind and with a driver shaken by the accident but determined to show his colleagues everything, we began with our one non-battlefield visit, the St Bernardus Brewery. We were late, so the tour wasn't possible, but they very kindly took us in, bedraggled by the crash, showed us a very informative presentation, and let us taste their excellent beers. Oh, hang on a minute, not quite. Let's not forget that Muggins here was driving, so whilst Zoë zanily zoned in on her zesty wheatbeer and Jack jostled into his jaw a joyous dubbel, I could only conclude that the water was wet and sparkly. If this sounds, erm, bitter, well I really needed that beer!

I have tried the St Bernardus range since, of course. And a fine range it is. The nearby St Sixtus Monastery decided not to sell its beer outside the monastery walls, which is probably the best reason I can think of to 'find God' and join their sect. The nearby cheesemaker was allowed to brew it under license and so the St Bernardus Brewery was born, now producing beers as close as possible to the neighbouring abbey's ales.

I've been on lots of trips around Flanders, more than one expertly arranged by Visit Flanders, the tourist board responsible for promoting tourism to the Flemish speaking region of Belgium. We've visited great artisan breweries, my favourite memory being at De Dolle Brouwers (The Mad Brewers) near Diksmuide. Their beers are amazing. The Oerbier (original beer) sticks in my mind at 9% alcohol. But the star of the show was the mad brewing brothers' granny, a feisty and funny 90 year old lady, who came out to give us a little talk about her longevity. She only ate pulses and raw things, like raw vegetables and berries. And only drank beer. She has been a big influence on my life, mad granny, as I've adopted the second part of her lifestyle. I hope I make it to 90.

Behind time and with a free morning the following day, we decided to use that free time to return to Poperinge. Heading through Ypres (or Ieper locally in Flemish) we began at the spot just outside the town dubbed 'Hellfire Corner' back then, a perilous place monitored by German guns. Nearby is the Hooge Crater Museum. If you haven't been, whilst the crater doesn't exist anymore, it is a good little museum filled with artefacts found in the surrounding fields. Nice people too, with a neat café. Just a short walk along the way is a field with original trenches. You are free to wander but encouraged to leave a Euro in a box by the gate.

Crossing back over to the west of town, we visited the Brandhoek New Military Cemetery. Amongst the graves, beautifully maintained by the Commonwealth War Graves Commission, is that of the remarkable Captain Dr Noel Chavasse, one of only three people to be decorated with the Victoria Cross twice. The doctor's bravery was in saving the lives of others whilst constantly putting his own life in peril. To visit such a place, honouring such a person, is a humbling experience and your own trials and tribulations, dented hire car included, begin to fade into insignificance.

The wind whistling through Zoë's door was all the air-conditioning we needed as the little Renault rattled over to the Essex Farm Cemetery. Also an Advanced Dressing Station of the Canadian Field Artillery during the Second Battle of Ypres, this is a place synonymous with the poet John McCrae, who reportedly wrote the poem 'In Flanders Fields' after witnessing his friend's burial there.

Next stop Tyne Cot near Passchendaele, the largest CWG cemetery in the world with a Memorial to the Missing and nearly 12,000 graves, roughly two thirds of which are unnamed. The scale of this gleaming white memorial brings home the sacrifice of a generation. I had been before and I've been back since. Endless rows of unnamed headstones. The sadness becomes no less intense.

With my half-German friend and colleague shivering in the autumnal breeze on the backseat, there was one final visit I wanted to make. It had been a thought-provoking part of a Visit Flanders educational tour I'd previously made, Langemark German Cemetery, a dark and brutal contrast in the day's fading light to the glistening white memorials of remembrance at Tyne Cot.

There aren't many German war cemeteries in Belgium. In those that do exist the headstones are of a darker stone and flat to the ground. There is no triumph here. On the memorial at Langemark is the inscription 'Deutschland muss leben, und wenn wir sterben müssen' or 'Germany must live, even if we have to die'. Immediately beyond it, leading to the touching sculpture of the four mourning soldiers by Emil Krieger, is a mass grave containing the remains of nearly 25,000 poor souls. These numbers are inconceivable, aren't they?

My Flanders trips would be the last ones for that company, as I eventually reached agreement with a new employer. There would be less time away from home, but more responsibility as I would be charged with running the business, a smaller rail tour operator. This emotional rollercoaster of a day, however, ended at the Menin Gate in Ypres, a triumphal arch and a Memorial to the Missing of the British & Commonwealth forces. The daily ritual at 8pm, the Last Post Ceremony, is the town's tribute to those who fell in the unthinkable hell of the trenches to preserve Belgium's freedom. I've been coming here since last century and the emotions are still as raw. Every time. The bugles, the silence, the goosebumps, the tears are all an important act of remembrance. After the day I'd had I don't mind telling you I found a quiet spot for a little moment to myself.

You know that feeling when you wake from a glorious but exhausted sleep into a bright new day? When you momentarily remember the car crash, the dented door and it was probably just part of your dream, wasn't it? Only to car crash back into reality. Yes, that one. I'd have some explaining to do at the car hire place in Lille before catching our afternoon Eurostar back to St Pancras, but first we'd better tick off yesterday's unfinished business.

Poperinge is a small town just west of Ypres. Known as 'Pops' to the Allied soldiers, its location in battlefield terms meant that it was just behind the lines, the place soldiers came to recover, to make merry even, from the infernal hell a few miles away. Driving alongside the flat farmland you can't fail to notice fields with umpteen poles supported by cables. On these structures grow the local star ingredient. You see, 'Pops' is king of the hops!

Once you've visited the Hop Museum, based in the town's former weigh-house, sampling the strong and fantastically hoppy Poperings Hommelbier, or maybe water if you are the now increasingly embittered designated driver, there are a couple of thought-provoking battlefield sites to visit too. At the town hall is the 'Shot at Dawn' exhibition, featuring the cell in which 'deserters', usually men suffering from shell-shock, spent their last night before an example was made of them the following day at the nearby execution pole. Shot by their own comrades instead of receiving compassion for the illness they were suffering. The pole in the courtyard is a stark reminder.

I'll just leave here the story of Herbert Morris of the West Indian Regiment, who signed up for what I presume he perceived would be an adventure in an exotic land far from his home in Jamaica. Shell-shocked and disorientated by the guns, Herbert absconded twice and was inevitably caught both times. Court martialled the second time, his death sentence confirmed by Field Marshall Haig, Herbert was first paraded in front of his regiment, then in the early hours of 20 September 1917 was shot at dawn by a firing squad of ten soldiers, seven of whom were West Indian. He was just 17.

Talbot House is a great antidote to the harrowing history contained within the arable furrows of the surrounding fields. When Poperinge was the garrison town of the British Army, chaplains Neville Talbot and Tubby Clayton set up an 'Every Man's Club', where soldiers could rest and revitalise themselves regardless of rank. It is still a very charming place to visit, a lovely museum, a little time capsule in which you can actually stay the night, tinkle the ivories on the house piano or just enjoy a social cuppa, which is exactly what we did.

We could have enjoyed our own relaxation and recreation a little while longer at Talbot House, but we had a Eurostar to catch, a knackered car to drop off and time was starting to get tight. With the minutes until departure from Lille Europe ticking away, the sat nav took us straight across the cobbles of Lille's main square, juddering away, the door whistling a nice tune to us to remind us of the car's sorry state. It felt a bit like a scene from the film 'The Italian Job', only this was not Italy and let's hope my own job wouldn't be on the line when the repair bill arrived. At any rate, the Renault's door would be a nice job for a Lille panel beater. The battlefields of Flanders now distant, with minutes to go until departure we reached our own final battle – the battle with Alamo! But I'm no fighter. I threw the keys on the counter, told them the car was kaput, then ran. Ran to the comfort of a beautiful train. And a beer. Santé!

Chapter 25 - Swiss Roll

The symmetry seemed perfect. It was ten years on from that initial trip with the Swiss Tourist Board which had switched me from coaches to trains. Ten years of train travel all over the world, but rarely to Switzerland. After a few months with my new smaller company, my first trip for them would take me back to Switzerland on a familiarisation visit with the Swiss Tourist Board. Little did I know that it would also be my last trip anywhere, for a while anyway.

It began with a new experience. Regular SBB Inter City trains took us to Chur, that great Swiss junction town, for the climb to Arosa. The Arosabahn is operated by Rhaetitian Railways, world famous for its blue riband tourist train experiences, the Bernina Express and the Glacier Express, which also operate out of Chur. It is easy to see why the Arosa Railway is overlooked amidst such inspiring company, but it is a really nice ride in its own right.

The Arosabahn trundles first through the quaint Old Town of Chur before dawdling out into the fresh mountain air on a single track that climbs over 1000 metres in just 26 km through an unspoilt natural paradise. Between Langwies and Litzirüti the 284 metre long Langwieser Viaduct crosses the River Plessur, the line's most famous structure amongst 41 bridges and 19 tunnels. Arosa, reached in around an hour from Chur, whilst being the end of the line, is a mountain resort that deserves more than the one night we spent there.

There is only one way back to Chur by rail, but we spent pleasant moments strolling through the Old Town, checking out hotels. Despite being far from the oldest in the group, I was perturbed to be lagging at the back. Unusually fatigued, I put it down to altitude, before forgetting about it as we joined the Glacier Express from Chur to Andermatt, then descending to Lake Lucerne on an exact replica of that previous trip ten years earlier. My night's sleep in Lucerne was obliterated by an itchy body rash that appeared from nowhere, prompting me to shower in the middle of the night, change nightshirt, strip the bed, blaming some unknown detergent or other. Throughout all those years of being away from home, only in Washington DC had I felt ill. Something wasn't quite right here, but I just couldn't work out what it was.

The following day is a blur. It must have begun with a train journey from Lucerne to Interlaken over the Brünig Pass, a very beautiful rail journey. I have been along the route quite a few times and would never be blasé about such a thing, but I just don't remember it. In Interlaken we definitely toured the town's proud streets on a horse and carriage on a sadly cold and grey day, before visiting the Ballenberg Open Air Museum near Lake Brienz. I remember this part of the day because we did a kind of 'Swiss Olympics', playing traditional Swiss games like throwing a hoop at a pole and hammering a nail into a piece of wood. How could you forget the excitement of competitive nail hammering?!

I know how we got to Wengen. I vaguely remember being in the junction station village of Lauterbrunnen, the roofs glistening from a recent rain shower. We will have reached Lauterbrunnen from Interlaken Ost on the Berner Oberland Bahn. Lauterbrunnen serves two other lines, the Bergbahn Lauterbrunnen-Mürren, more of which in the next chapter, and the Wengeneralpbahn. We will have taken the latter to Wengen and our next hotel. I say 'will have' because again I don't remember.

Three Wengen hotel visits, dinner together as a group, skin blotchy and struggling to stay awake, wondering what on Earth was wrong with me, our hotelier for this night arranged to show us around his hotel. By now it was around 11 o'clock at night. As we waited for him to collect the room keys from reception, night suddenly arrived early for me.

I woke, gradually lifting my head from the table I had managed to reach before collapsing. A taxi was waiting to take me to the local doc, who had been raised from his own slumber. This being Switzerland, the doc performed an ECG and did blood tests. This being Switzerland the blood test results were available immediately. The doc confirmed that it wasn't a heart attack, but the test results required me to seek medical help urgently on my return home. High in the Alps in the early hours of the morning, unwell, alone but unwilling to burden my wife back home with my worry, I put myself to bed wondering what on earth was wrong with me. It sounds dramatic, but as I fell asleep I had the notion that I may never wake up.

I was severely anaemic. What followed was a year of tests for this cancer and that cancer. Eventually, after months and months of prodding, Crohns was diagnosed, something that can be managed. The collapse, followed by the realisation that this crazy, hardcore travelling man was breakable, led me to consider that travel was out of the question for a while. Eventually my confidence returned, but not before a year or more without leaving these shores for fear of being stuck somewhere remote on my own with no medical help, all for the sake of making holidays. Sometimes reality hits you with a thud. There are more important things in life than the Wengeneralpbahn. Those three women in my life back home, for starters.

Chapter 26 - Secret Switzerland

'Sorry. The upper deck is for First Class ticket holders only.'
These were the words of the attendant on one of the BLS vessels criss-crossing between idyllic villages on the banks of Lake Thun. To be fair we were a little bedraggled. It was day one of a family camping holiday by Lake Thun and we had sailed across to Spiez to raid Lidl. Having walked up the hill at Spiez, then back down armed with Lidl carrier bags, we probably did not look first class. He was positioned at the stairwell, this officious chap, to keep riff-raff like us off the genteel upper deck.

'We are First Class,' I replied with a wry smile, showing him our First Class Swiss Passes, before we dragged our Lidl bags upstairs and plonked ourselves in the chairs on the sundeck. It felt like a subtle but very satisfying two finger salute to the man in uniform, the establishment, the status quo.

This would be 2016, a full two years on. After my Swiss roll and subsequent cancer scare, followed by trying to compute the repercussions of living and travelling with Crohns, I didn't go anywhere very far away. I sent colleagues on trips instead, before finally accepting that I should start to carry on with my normal life, perhaps slowed down a tad, and this time maybe taking my loved ones with me where possible to share the highs and lows of the adventure.

Crohns, in case you are not aware, is a debilitating bowel disease causing chronic pain and discomfort in most sufferers, often requiring big changes in diet and lifestyle, plus heavy medication to control it. Mine is a severe case in one sense, managed by weekly injections, but I am otherwise asymptomatic. Only the anaemia that caused my collapse in Switzerland (and probably the near collapse in Washington DC) plus chronic fatigue affect my otherwise healthy life. I am a lucky man.

Armed with our Swiss Passes, the passport that unlocks most doors on the Swiss transport system, we would spend a few nights camping by Lake Thun, then three nights with a good hotelier friend of mine by Lake Lucerne. Amidst the simple fun of swimming in the lake, relaxing by Interlaken's open air swimming pool, fantastically framed by the Bernese Oberland, I had surreptitiously arranged to drag the clan up mountains on railways not featured by anyone else in their brochures.

'Are you secretly planning a brand-new tour during our family holiday?' asked Mrs C in a resigned manner.

'Erm, what do you think?'

Taking in relatively unknown mountain railways, the eventual tour would be called 'Secret Switzerland', hilariously dubbed 'Secret Squirrel' in the office after a 1960s kids' cartoon series. Secret Squirrel was the buck-toothed James Bond of the rodent world. More of which later, but let's start at Basel Airport, where we joined the Swiss rail system. Skirting the southern shore of Lake Thun, I had made sure we were seated left of the carriage. Between Spiez and Interlaken the views open up, the lake glistening in the late August sun, backed by the mountains we'd explore over the coming days. Looking across the lake, the holiday had begun.

We hopped onto the BLS ship for the first time, upstairs of course, meandering gently back and forth across Lake Thun to Beatenbucht. Here we met our first off-the-beaten-track mountain railway, the Niederhorn. Actually, it's two rail experiences in one, the first by funicular to Beatenberg village, where the Beatenberg-Niederhorn cable car waits to whisk you the rest of the way to the summit. And what a summit. What a start. It was a clear day and from the peak at 1950 metres above sea level there is a sheer cliff with views out to the Justistal valley. Turn around to the direction just travelled, Lake Thun is distant below, surrounded by the Bernese Alps in all their glory, not least the three great snowcapped peaks of Eiger, Mönch and Jungfrau.

The next trip is a little better known. Mrs C calls it 'Schniegen Schnagen' but its real name is actually the Schynige Platte Railway. A four-minute journey from Interlaken Ost station brought us to the village of Wilderswil. It is a line that dates all the way back to 1893 and still sometimes using steam traction. Our regular service climbed and meandered through woods and alpine meadows, with great views of Interlaken and its surrounding lakes, Thun and Brienz. We took photographs of incredible scenery, with another train in the distance, possibly good enough for the brochure. Then, a minute later, those photos would be superseded by even better scenery, such is the raw rocky beauty of this particular great railway journey.

Coming towards the summit Schynige Platte station some 7km later, an altitude just higher than yesterday's Niederhorn at 1,987 metres, the great peaks of the Bernese Oberland, the omnipresent Eiger, Mönch and Jungfrau, come into view. There is plenty to do at the top as well, with a restaurant and alpine garden and lovely walks. My kids always had a good nose for finding the playground and this splendid mountain stroll led us to their highest altitude see-saw.

Onto the Schilthorn. I've been told more than once that the Schilthorn round-trip is more enjoyable than the Jungfraubahn. It has several elements and its altitude means that you actually get to see the great peaks Eiger, Mönch and Jungfrau close up across the valley. That's what I've been told anyway. The first time I went up there, the day before that collapse two years previously, we had been met with thick fog. So here was an opportunity to revisit and, fingers crossed, to wallow in the views from the top of Piz Gloria, the revolving restaurant at the Schilthorn's summit, 2,970 metres above sea level. It was famously featured in the 1969 James Bond movie 'On Her Majesty's Secret Service', the only one with George Lazenby as Bond. And, boy, do they milk their 007 connections to the edge of Bond's fragile death-defying life.

A train took us from Interlaken to Lauterbrunnen, that station connecting to several of the world's greatest mountain railway experiences. A postbus took us further along the valley to Stechelberg. From Stechelberg at 867 metres the first cable car rises as far as Mürren (1,638 metres). Here you switch onto another cable car for the final longer ascent to Schilthorn and Piz Gloria at nearly 3,000 metres. The whole experience takes about half an hour.

It didn't look good during the ascent, visibility gradually decreasing. At the top.....it was just thick fog! Once again I sat with a coffee in the revolving restaurant that gives 360 degree panoramas, with more visibility in my murky cup than out of the windows. But we had good fun with 007, Mrs C posing as a Bond Girl and with the slapstick 007 sound effects in the loos. Was that a gunshot I heard when I pressed the bog handle? I may have pressed it quite a few times just to make sure. I like your style, Mr Bond.

Shaken, but not stirred, I re-emerged from my highest altitude mountain water closet. The clouds weren't clearing, so we continued our round trip, taking the alternative route back to Lauterbrunnen. Back down in Mürren, instead of switching onto the other cable car to Stechelberg, we took a wander through the village instead. The clouds were lifting slightly and if we squinted we could maybe see Eiger, Mönch and Jungfrau, but, hey, to be fair we were kind of seeing them most days anyway from one vantage point or another.

Mürren, though, is an exquisite alpine village, houses adorned with flowers and with a different railway at the other end, the BLM. The Bergbahn Lauterbrunnen Mürren takes you down from 1,638 metres to Grutschalp at 1,486 metres along a route just over 4 km in length. At Grutschalp the cable car makes the big descent to Lauterbrunnen over the final 1 ½ km to the valley floor. It's an exhilarating round trip filled with thrills and spills, lots of different experiences and with a bona fide attraction at the top. I cannot wait to return. Third time lucky, maybe?

The final mountain had been staring at us from across Lake Thun all week. A mysterious perfect pyramid shaped summit lured me to drag the family on one last excursion. They were weary by now. There was a bit of dissent in the camp. I caught a little sense of potential mutiny, particularly amongst the younger travellers. So we did a deal. If we could climb Niesen in the morning, then we would spend the afternoon at Interlaken's Bödelibad, the open-air pool with an amazing name and even more amazing backdrop.

We took a train to Mülenen in the valley bottom beneath the pyramid. The Niesen funicular opened in 1910 and runs for 3 ½ km from Mülenen to the summit, a journey that takes around 25 minutes with one interchange at Schwandegg. The summit at Niesen is 2,336 metres above sea-level. It's a hell of a climb!

As the funicular glides up the mountain you can't fail to see steps alongside the track, which are for the use of maintenance staff. There are 11,674 in total, comprising the world's largest staircase. I discovered that something takes place here called the 'Niesenlauf', a public race to the top. 11,674 steps! As I write this I can feel another blackout coming on.

At the top there is a large viewing platform. It was one of those days where we had ridden through the clouds, basking in the warm glow of bright sunshine at the peak, superior in the knowledge that those suckers below the sea of cloud were suffering an overcast morning. Dad had made the right choice today and we were in no hurry to leave the rays behind. It just got better and better though, with the clouds gradually dispersing, first offering glimpses, then full view of the whole region, Lake Thun's azure waters one side and an incredible collection of snow-capped mountains to the other.

A relaxing afternoon in the Bödelibad kept everyone amused. It is a beautiful place, built in 1930 and subject to a preservation order. Top tip from dad: the railway line passes just round the back of the period changing cabins and the top of the waterslide is a great vantage point for watching passing trains. At this point I can hear my wife and kids cry, 'We give up!'

Chapter 27 - Erin on the Side of Caution

'How are ya?' asked the stranger as we walked past him.
'Fine thanks.'
'Where are ya from?'
'Leeds,' came our nervous answer.

A couple of tense moments followed. It had seemed like a good idea. On holiday on the Antrim Coast, but obviously also trying out some ideas for a new tour that would include the most scenic railway journey on the island of Ireland, we had dropped the car off that morning in Coleraine. This in itself had thrown up a quandary. The terraced-housed streets around the station on which we could park were daubed with the union flag. We figured we'd be okay to park our car with clearly British mainland number plates outside a loyalist's house? It would be there all day, but hopefully we wouldn't take up their space and incur anyone's wrath.

The Belfast to Derry-Londonderry line really gets exciting after Coleraine, which explains why we chose to take it from there. Operated by Translink, you need to sit to the right of the train when travelling westwards, as the route skirts the coast. From Coleraine the line runs alongside the River Bann before passing through Castlerock and Downhill tunnels, the longest in Ireland. After the coastal village of Castlerock it passes the Binevenagh Mountain, the track then running alongside the empty golden sands of Benone Strand, with expansive views of beaches and waves crashing in from the Atlantic Ocean under big Irish skies. Well, that's how it was for us as we were blessed with sunny early-autumn weather.

Derry-Londonderry station is a bit of a walk from the centre, but a free shuttle bus whisks you across the River Foyle in no time to a city with a troubled past, clear divisions still but one with a lot going for it. We liked the city and the walls were a great place to start exploring. It's from these walls that many tourists get their safe vantage point views of Derry-Londonderry's divided communities. There's a panoramic view of the Catholic Nationalist Bogside, as well as a glimpse of the Protestant Loyalist Fountain estate. The latter is the last small enclave of Loyalists living within the city's Catholic West Bank that includes the city centre, with most Loyalists now residing on the East Bank across the river. As it is surrounded by an ominous cage-like security fence, I left my wife and daughters to have a wander into the Fountain, with its red, white and blue painted kerbs, though I didn't venture far. A foreboding mural at the entrance to the estate, just outside the city wall, harks back not only to the Siege of Derry (1688-9), but also to the estate's current encircled situation – 'Londonderry West Bank Loyalists Still Under Siege – No Surrender.'

Whilst I did not feel particularly comfortable as a tourist in embattled Fountain, the part of the Catholic Bogside that is visible from the city walls is very much on the tourist trail. With two history-mad daughters in their mid-teens I figured that we shouldn't shy away from part of our history. We were here, at the scene of a relatively recent important and highly controversial historical event. And so we left the walls and headed towards the Bogside, scene of Bloody Sunday. Immediately we were stopped by a passer-by wishing to know where we were from. My half-Irish wife is called Maeve, named after the warrior queen, Maedhbh of Connacht, who went through husbands like nobody's business. Our eldest daughter is called Erin, named after the Irish word for Ireland itself! Our youngest is Clare, which is self-explanatory in this context. But amidst their blue eyes and delicate, pale freckled features there's still no disguising a Yorkshire accent!

The tense moments didn't last long though. Our inquisitor, Sean, told us we were perfectly safe, to have a look at the murals and to look out for the first name on the Bloody Sunday Memorial down in the

Bogside below, commemorating the 14 who were killed on 30th January 1972. Patrick Doherty had been Sean's work colleague. He had seen him at work on the Friday, but he was never to return. Sean was on his way into town to meet his wife for lunch, was already behind time, but was happy to explain a little more about Bloody Sunday. He told us the marches were predominantly about Civil Rights really rather than sectarian at that point, Derry-Londonderry being an impoverished corner of the island, cut off from its natural hinterland by the border, subject to a brain drain and a distinct lack of investment. Opportunities had been few and far between, particularly for Catholics. We thanked Sean for his time, suggested that he'd be in trouble with his wife if he spent much longer giving us an impromptu guided tour. Hell, I even suggested that he take himself off to Visit Derry, the local tourist board, and sign up for them as a living, breathing guide with first-hand experience of those times that we tritely describe as 'the Troubles'.

The Bogside is an unnerving eye-opener, its painted murals harking back to a paramilitary past and trouble still ongoing. Yet within all of this we were still greeted by an Ireland we've come to love. Your worries and fears are disarmed in an instant by charming, friendly,

hospitable people like Sean. And this is a city that provokes a lot of thought. We walked back to the station over the Peace Bridge across the Foyle, linking the Catholic West Bank or Cityside with the Protestant East Bank or Waterside. It was opened in 2011 ahead of the city's stint as UK City of Culture in 2013, an event which increased visitor numbers dramatically. My girls have since grown to adore the tv series, 'Derry Girls' and, when I ask them to which destination they'd like to return, Derry-Londonderry is high up, if not top of the list! How banjaxed is that?!

Chapter 28 - Never Mind the Bolagets, Here's the Wet Whistles

'**O**h….erm….are you sure you have definitely booked in for tonight?'

The hotel manager was flustered on the phone. This was Sunday, after all, and I normally stayed on Mondays. I was standing outside the hotel's closed up reception with no sign of life inside. I won't name the hotel as it still exists and despite its little, let's say, idiosyncrasies, they are nice people and I enjoyed a prolonged period staying there one night a week during a my stint with my new company.

It's a grand looking building on the edge of town, an old manor house with a 1970s built annexe, pub and leisure club. After my employer had initially plonked me at the cheapest B&B they could find, a mile away from any pub or eaterie, without including breakfast to save money (I suppose that makes it a B?), the following year's success allowed me to go up in the world. With around thirty bedrooms and facilities on-site it had sounded perfect. And I would get breakfast too!

The first time I stayed there I rocked through the craters in the car park and rocked up to reception, only to find it closed. I found out that the hotel's very few guests entered through the pub to check in at the bar. When I first went through to the pool, part of an efficient leisure club that had seen better days but mostly still functioned, the attendant was watching 'The Hotel Inspector' with the very watchable Alex

Polizzi. The whole premise of the show is to rescue failing hotels from the brink. Having seen my room, the only one of their thirty rooms occupied that night, with its 1980s patterned carpet, thin yellow curtains, dusty lampshade and singing plumbing in the bathroom, I had a little chuckle to myself at the irony.

But this wasn't the first stay. God knows, despite its faults I must have loved that place so much that I stayed every week for nearly three years, often the only guest amidst all the unsold rooms and with a breakfast service seemingly just for me. No, this was a Sunday night though, a break from the norm which clearly had thrown into disarray the hotel's schedule of mostly having one guest a week, but arriving on a Monday night. The manager looked perturbed when he arrived in person to open up.

'Which room do you want? Take your pick.'

I opted for my favourite room 21, a huge bedroom with creaky floorboards and a ceramic teddy bear toilet brush holder, but with the advantage of a fully working shower.

'I'm afraid the kitchen is closed on Sundays and so are the pool and gym. The pub is open though and we'll be open until late. If you need anything, I'll be on the bar. It's just me here today. Oh......will you be needing breakfast tomorrow morning and, if so, what time?'

I could see him grimacing at this point and so asked whether, having run the bar until closing time, the manager would also be forced to get up for breakfast duty for his unexpected sole guest? When he nodded sheepishly I offered to make my own breakfast if he would show me where everything was in the hotel's kitchen.

'Are you sure? Okay, go on then.'

So there you have it. I've stayed in hundreds of hotels over the years, checking them out for customers. This particular one, for very obvious reasons, I would only reserve for myself, but at 7am the following morning I trotted into a hotel kitchen to make some toast, cereal and a cup of coffee, sat down to eat it in the breakfast room, then dutifully returned to the kitchen to wash my pots. At that point the housekeeper arrived and caught me in the act with the tea towel.

'What the hell are you doing in here?! You're a paying guest! This is a hotel! You shouldn't have to make your own breakfast!'

During those years, a period in which I had to come to terms with the idea of not being an unbreakable hardcore crazy travel guy, learning to accept the limitations caused by my Crohns (as well as the onset of middle-age), I took a conscious decision not to travel too far too often with work. Besides, my office was a two hour drive across the glorious Peak District and I would make that return journey every week. Then came an offer of a trip that I simply could not refuse, my first big work adventure for around four years.

The pre-show tours for the Visit Sweden event had been tempting. There was an experience of a Sami camp, for example. I chose to make my own pre-tour. It's not a holiday, after all; this is work!

I would have less than 24 hours in Denmark's lovely capital, Copenhagen. I had planned, planned, then planned again before deciding what to do. The bottom line was that my daughter's birthday could not be missed. I was due in Umeå on the edge of Swedish Lapland, had a couple of unseen things in southern Sweden to check out ahead of a group travelling a few months later, plus an empty pad to plot out the following few years' highly lucrative Scandinavian programmes for my then employer, something completely new I had produced for them. Blimey, that pad was full by the end of the trip. Due to another change of companies a few months later, a new job back home in Yorkshire, in my pad those tours will remain. For now at least.

Moving to Airedale Tours later that year (2018), not a recognised rail holiday company, I decided to start writing. I suppose it was an attempt to get rail out of my system. It didn't work. I wrote and wrote, but my passion for rail holidays just intensified as I relived my experiences. I once promised a German company a German-speaking tour manager for a ten-day tour of Wales's railways I had designed for them. When it came to the crunch I picked up the clipboard and guided it myself. It was challenging, presenting your own product in person for ten days in a foreign language, but also one of the most rewarding things I have ever done.

There will be more of this (and Wales) in the next chapters. Back to what would become the last trip for my previous company, I would fly into Copenhagen for a night, then the following late afternoon hop into Sweden across 'The Bridge', featured in the Nordic noir crime thriller of the same name. A night in Linköping, then missing out Stockholm, already well known from previous trips, I would spend Saturday night in Gävle. My journey would then head up the Swedish coast to Umeå for a couple of nights. On my way back I would stay a night in Uppsala, just north of Stockholm, before flying home.

I had used the Imperial Hotel in Copenhagen many times before with good reviews, however, having never stayed there personally, enjoyed a night there. I had lined up three further hotel visits the following morning, just in case the Imperial was not right for us, but still somehow managed to see as many of the sights of Copenhagen as possible, on foot, in the May sunshine.

I decided to walk all the way to the Little Mermaid statue, some 4 km away. Sure, a good public transport system is available, but sometimes the best way to see a city is on foot. And the weather helped. I took a quick detour round the side of Central Station to Tivoli Gardens, Copenhagen's famous amusement park. Opened in 1843 the Tivoli is the world's second-oldest and features the thrills and spills of rides, as well as pleasure gardens, a concert hall and open air theatre amongst a wealth of other attractions.

Town Hall Square (Rådhuspladsen) was having a bit of a facelift at the time, so I hotfooted along the Strøget, the main shopping street and one of Europe's longest. At the very pleasant Kongens Nytorv (King's New Square) suddenly one of Copenhagen's true gems just appears from amidst the bustle of urban city life. The New Harbour, or Nyhavn, is far from new, dating from the 17th century. The charming waterfront, flanked by townhouses, cafés and bars would have been a truly lovely maritime place to while away a couple of hours, but those couple of hours I just did not have to spare.

My self-guided walking tour did not get any worse. Next up along the route to the Little Mermaid was Amalienborg Palace, a complex of four identical royal palaces encircling a courtyard. Incredibly, it is perfectly okay to wander through. Things are very relaxed here, with the palaces protected by the Royal Life Guards. A little further, the pentagon-shaped Citadel (or Kastellet) is one of Europe's best-preserved fortresses. There's a little church within the citadel and a windmill amongst a park that makes for a really pleasant walk away from the crowds.

Of course, the crowds are not far away. They probably miss the citadel on their way to the big attraction, as tiny as she is in comparison. Coaches pull in and out of the quayside, the crowds line the quay to take a snapshot of the Little Mermaid. Den Lille Havfrue, unveiled in 1913, depicts one of Hans Christian Andersen's most famous fairy tales and has become the city's most famous landmark.

There was one last place I wanted to see on my whistle-stop tour of Copenhagen, Christiania. A thorn in the side of the Danish authorities since 1971, Christiania in the suburb of Christianshavn had previously been military buildings. After years of disuse the area was broken into, civilians conquering a 'forbidden military zone', and became world-famous as 'Freetown Christiania', a centre for the hippy and autonomous movements. Over the decades the relationship between Christiania residents and the authorities has been like one of the rollercoaster rides downtown at the Tivoli, with open cannabis trading at one point on the so-called 'Pusher Street' and the accompanying territorial feuds that can come with the trade of illicit substances. Nowadays Christiania is bizarrely one of Copenhagen's most-visited attractions, with tourists safely wandering through the hippy commune, surrounded by the whiff of ganja, taking selfies of an alternative lifestyle theme-park.

From the depths of Kobenhavn Hovedbanegard, or Copenhagen Central to me and you, I found SJ's swanky X2000, which would run direct to Stockholm, via Malmö and my next port of call, Linköping. SJ, which stands for Statens Järnvägar, is the Swedish national rail operator and the tilting X2000 trains are designed to reach speeds up to 200 kmph on routes linking the country's major cities, including Malmö and Stockholm, with several services a day linking Copenhagen to Sweden across the bridge.

The bridge? Ah yes, that bridge. The one that links Denmark to Sweden. The bridge featured in the Nordic noir television crime drama called, erm, 'The Bridge'. Its actual name is the Øresund Bridge as it crosses a strait of the same name. The bridge itself is only part of the crossing though, as the journey begins with the 4km long Drogden

Tunnel from the Danish island of Amager to Peberholm, an artificial island, before resurfacing and crossing the remaining 8km by bridge.

Alas, the rails run on the lower tier of the structure beneath the motorway, so whilst the motorists above you bask in the glow of sea and sky as far as the eye can see, rail passengers only get to see the sea. This slight feeling of anti-climax was broken by an unusual occurrence these days travelling through Europe, an in-train passport check.

Southern Sweden is fairly flat, so I sat back as the tilting train whizzed, the power socket and wifi provided even in Standard Class enabling me to work. Linköping, whilst being Sweden's fifth largest city, has a really pleasant centre, dominated by its cathedral. It is a great base for exploring central southern Sweden's canals. Having got caught in monsoon-style weather on the short walk between station and hotel, clothes hung up to dry, I pondered the significance of this trip, the first major foreign jaunt on my own since my collapse four years earlier. That night in Wengen clearly had changed my outlook on life and, whilst this was an excitement I missed, I missed my family too. I thought I had better console myself with a beer, just for medicinal purposes, you'll understand, so went in search of a shop.

You live and learn. This was, what, my third or fourth visit to Sweden, yet a revelation was about to occur. A fundamental one too for the sole traveller. Perusing the shelves of the shop, the beer selection was poor. What's more, looking at the alcohol content on the tins reminded me of those heady days at school, underage drinking with my mates on the bench by the football field, getting squiffy at the mere smell of a can of Skol.

I decided not to bother and instead consoled myself with a bench by the rather wonderful green oasis of gardens in the city centre maintained by the Trädgårdsföreningen, Linköping's Horticultural Society. No can of Skol tonight though!

The wonders of the internet. Laptop cranked up, hotel limited free wifi activated, I discovered that Swedish alcohol laws are a little complicated. Or uncomplicated. I'm not actually sure which is correct. Your average shop is allowed to sell some alcoholic beverages, though to a maximum alcoholic content of 3.5%. Mmm, so if your taste is for anything other than almost non-alcohol lager, then you need to find a Systembolaget. A what?!

A Systembolaget. In Sweden alcohol sales, in shops at least, are run by a state monopoly chain of liquor stores called Systembolaget. There isn't one on every corner and they have strict opening hours. Having missed the boat with Linköping's liquor store, I used my last seconds of hotel free wifi researching the vital information required for my next three overnight stays, the whereabouts and opening times of the Systembolaget!

Next stop Gävle, sitting north of Stockholm on the line up to my eventual destination on the doorstep of Swedish Lapland. A change in Stockholm would have enabled me to use the high speed X2000s further, but instead I plumped for SJ's older Intercity service, direct from Linköping to Gävle via Stockholm, a journey of 3 ½ hours.

Gävle of a Saturday afternoon is quiet. Bag dropped at my room in the lovely Grand Hotel, show round completed with the poor sod on Saturday duty, I did the necessary planning for the evening. With the Eurovision Song Contest taking place, usually a family spectacle back home, I found Gävle's Systembolaget.

It might seem an odd choice to stay in Gävle rather than Stockholm. But I had already been to Stockholm a few times and, in any case, I was putting together rail holidays and Gävle is the home of Sweden's National Railway Museum or Järnvägsmuseet. Or it would be if it were not closed for long-term renovation, with the reopening continually being put back, 2022 at the earliest according to the latest. They still operate day excursions from the yard though and the lovely people there would have opened especially for me, had I been able to arrive earlier, what with it being Saturday and all. Not to worry as I took a wander down the lanes to find it and to take snaps of the train hall, the roundhouse and station through the fences with my telephoto lens. It houses a vast collection of locomotives and carriages, around 300 in total. Definitely a place on my list of future trips.

Away from the excitement of peering at distant railway sheds through a barbed wire fence, Gävle is a lovely town. Its centrepiece is an avenue, tree-lined with gardens running down the middle, with the city's theatre and town hall as standing proudly as book ends. A beautiful early summer's walk by the river brought me to the sculpture of the "Five Musical Geniuses" with the city's music hall on the opposing bank. A wander through the cobbled streets of the preserved Old Town or Gamla Gefle brought me to the Joe Hill Museum, commemorating the life of Hill, who grew up in that humble little house.

Joel Emmanuel Hägglund, known later as Joe Hill, emigrated to America and became involved in trade unionism, writing songs and poems about the hard life of immigrant and itinerant workers in the States, the most famous of which are 'There is power in a union' and 'The preacher and the slave'. Hill was executed by firing squad in 1915, following a controversial trial in which he was accused of the murder of two men, including a policeman, in a grocery store. Hill had turned up at the doctor's the same evening with a gunshot wound.

Back at the hotel with a solo evening of Eurovision and Systembolaget Swedish craft beer, texting home with my scores after each performance, one thing became very clear. Eurovision just isn't the same without my girls. Nor is it the same with an earnest Swedish commentary that you cannot understand instead of Graham Norton's dry and sometimes wicked put-downs. Thank goodness for Systembolaget, my new favourite shop.

Sunday morning saw the final stretch of my journey north. It would take 5 ½ hours to reach my destination Umeå from Gävle, with a short-ish change in Sundsvall. The first couple of hours to Sundsvall would be on another sexy SJ X2000, changing onto a regional train for the remainder of the trip. Sweden is a vast country. The station names don't exactly trip off the tongue. Söderhamn, Härnösand, Örnsköldsvik, Hörnefors. The scenery is a wilderness. It is a journey worth making, but one which needs a good book as a companion. Or the Thomas Cook European Rail Timetable and a notepad, for those of us plotting future rail adventures.

The train arrived on time into an Umeå basking in sunshine. With a couple of hours to spare until the opening event of the fair, I dropped my bag in my room, noting the automatic blinds on the panoramic window over Umeå city, and legged it to the Umeå Energi Arena. It was half-time in the Swedish regional third division game between

Umeå FC and Rynninge IK, the gates were open and so I just walked in.

Despite the May sun, snow was still piled behind one of the goals. I headed for the grandstand, a wonderful wooden structure. Some fans were enjoying a half-time barbeque and a beer or two on the concourse. I took a seat on the long wooden benches in the grandstand, counted the five or six strong Rynninge IK travelling army of supporters in the opposite stand and watched a goalless second half. Typical of my luck, the excitement had already passed before I got there, with Umeå holding onto a 2-1 lead.

As pleasant as Umeå is, it didn't feel like the true north. Although the city could be used as a base from which to explore nature, for me it would be destined to act as a stop-over on an adventure heading beyond the Arctic Circle. The Systembolaget was handy though and, work completed, I watched the late evening daylight through my panoramic window above the city, accompanied by a strong Swedish craft ale, before closing the shutters to sleep.

After a morning of hotel visits and meetings I left Umeå in the early afternoon sun, heading back along the same tracks. To mix things up I had booked the direct SJ X2000 tilting temptress of the tracks to arrive in my next stop, Uppsala, at around 8pm. To mix things up some more I had booked First Class. The price difference wasn't huge. And finally, to test the service to the full, I had reserved an on-board meal.

First Class on an X2000 I would highly recommend for the small upgrade cost. There is more space, with a configuration of two seats one side of the aisle and one seat on the other. The seat pitches are spacious and it is a comfortable experience as the train whizzes to Örnsköldsvik, Söderhamn and Härnösand. The meal? Well, to be safe and in line with the dietary requirements of my condition (no raw meat or fish), I chose a vegetarian option. Whilst a cold meal comprising seeds and pulses might not be to everyone's taste, it certainly was to mine. Delicious.

Why was I in Uppsala, a Swedish city 40 miles north of Stockholm and probably most famous for its university? It is the terminus of the Uppsala-Länna Jernväg, or Lennekatten Railway, a heritage steam journey that leaves Uppsala Östra (East) station, a piece of wry Swedish humour as East Station is actually on the far platform at Uppsala Central Station with a Lennekatten Railway ticket office. What follows is a 23-mile ride through the Uppsala plains, through the dense Vedyxa forest and past inviting lakes on its way to the Faringe, with its beautifully preserved wooden station building.

One of the joys of travel is finding a hidden gem. With the Lennekatten reconnoitred and the hotels within walking distance of the station visited, I ventured the short distance into Uppsala's historic centre. What I found was one of the most pleasant surprises in all my years of travelling. Hundreds of bikes parked along the riverside, pleasure parks, a tree-lined avenue leading to an imposing castle, botanical gardens and the domineering Domkyrka or cathedral, originating from the 13th century. It helps a place's appearance when the sun is beating down, but Uppsala was one of the most beautiful cities I had stumbled upon. And I found the Systembolaget too. Skål!

Chapter 29 - Saving Wales

'**M**y life changed in 1974 when I woke up an alcoholic.'

The older chap had boarded the Llangollen Steam Railway in Llangollen for our short afternoon trip to Carrog. He had never travelled on a heritage railway, but his friend is a member of the railway society and had given him a ticket.

The unassuming middle-aged woman, clearly a stranger but an enthusiastic regular of the line, had suggested that he take a seat on the right hand side for the views and towards the front of this front carriage to feel the power of the loco. They had started to talk.

The gentleman's conversation turned to how he dealt with his alcoholism by finding the 'Lord Jesus Christ', followed by a long monologue featuring words like 'sins', 'repent' and 'meeting your maker'.

'My life changed with Thomas the Tank Engine,' the woman eventually replied. 'Didn't we all have our lives changed by Thomas the Tank Engine?'

'No.'

It was a short response from the born again to a subject that wasn't about him and his incredible journey away from the demon booze, accompanied by 'the Lord Jesus Christ' himself.

The reformed alcoholic's phone rang. It was his wife.

'I've just met a young lady called Polly. She is a sinner.......'

At the end of the phone call Polly diplomatically suggested that she had dealt with her bad sins her own way and that she would keep her not so bad sins, such as chocolate.

'When you aren't working on the railway, what do you do?' asked the pious pensioner.

'I don't work on the railway,' responded Polly.

'Well, when you aren't volunteering on the railway, what do you do?'

'I'm not a volunteer. I just ride up and down. I've just bought some postcards of my beloved Foxcote Manor, number 7822. She is coming home to Llangollen next month. I will do anything for her. I've donated money to help her be repainted in Brunswick green,' explained Polly.

'Right.'

I was faced with two evangelists. One had saved himself through faith and there is nothing wrong with that, but for the zealous need to enforce a worldview on the rest of us 'sinners', based upon the superior knowledge of his own salvation. The other had saved herself through a love of steam trains and Foxcote Manor, 7822, in particular. One clearly had no interest in anyone else's passion. The other worshipped a false idol, and worse still, an idol that thundered from the earth, snorting great smoke fuelled from a devilish furnace.

Llangollen is a pretty town in an even prettier spot in the valley of the River Dee and Llangollen Canal. Travelling westwards, leaving Llangollen behind there is a short stop at Berwyn, with the oldest chain bridge in the world and Horseshoe Falls just a short walk away. The scenery then soon opens up on the right hand side. Next stop is Glyndyfrdwy, nestled between the Llantysilio and Berwyn mountain ranges and entwined with the story of Owain Glyndŵr, who from here announced himself Prince of Wales in 1400 and began a rebellion against English rule. With the extension to Corwen currently closed, journey's end was the charming Carrog station, where what Polly described to her new acquaintance as 'the matchbox loco' (it's to do with the oblong shape of the tank) performed its popular stunt of uncoupling, running along the parallel line to reattach itself to the now opposite end of the carriages, before performing the same journey in reverse.

The railway isn't the only attraction here. A couple of miles out of town lies a UNESCO World Heritage site, the Pontcysyllte Aqueduct. It is the tallest navigable aqueduct in the world and the longest in the

UK, stretching majestically across the Dee Valley. For those comfortable with heights you can walk across the towpath, watching the narrowboats gently nudging across the 'stream in the sky' or gazing across the near distance at the next engineering masterpiece, the Traphont Cefn railway viaduct.

As for me, this was a recce ahead of leading a group of German railway enthusiasts around Wales for my new employer, not strictly a rail travel company. I had begun writing this book in attempt to 'get rail out of my system', but it clearly did not work. I would be back with the group a month later to worship Polly's false idol, Foxcote Manor, 7822, a big Great Western loco, a snorting, clanking beautiful beast. No offence to Mr Born Again. I'm glad he dealt with his demons, though it is a bore to be inflicted with someone's own assumed and possibly unfounded moral superiority. So I stand with Polly on this one.

Chapter 30 - Love, Hope & Belief

'I hope your group won't be disappointed. We haven't got much!' Nikki is sitting at her laptop in the railway café, enjoying a little banter with the couple from northeastern England, who are tucking into a sandwich and a cuppa prepared by Margaret. They are waiting for the railway's General Manager, Mac, to return from his latest maintenance task to take them on the railway's miniature 'Pixie Line'.

Nikki knows her stuff. She hadn't been interested in railways, but in 2014 the Teifi Valley was on the brink and needed help. An accountant, she was brought in by Mac, who himself had been newly installed as General Manager, to help navigate the railway's dire financial situation.

I had driven through stunning mid-Wales from Llangollen to cover the heritage railways of South Wales for my forthcoming German group. Situated in a yard called Henllan Station in Newcastle Emlyn in west Wales, the Teifi Valley Railway has access to enough land to make an interesting, preserved heritage line and visitor attraction, which is exactly what it once was. A narrow-gauge railway running along a former standard gauge Great Western track bed, the Teifi Valley Railway first carried passengers in 1985 as a heritage railway. With extensions to the line, in its 2 mile long heyday it carried close to 30,000 tourists a year, although there exists 6 miles of potential track bed within the land owned by the society.

The beginning of the 2010s brought financial problems and upheaval. To cut a long story short, which Nikki did, the local businessman who had taken over the struggling café eventually took over the running of the railway too. What followed was a stripping of the railway's assets, as track was torn up, sleepers too, the locomotives eventually being replaced by a 'landtrain', a tractor pulling trailers. The real reason for the change was to exploit the woodland, felling trees from the Teifi Valley Railway's land and selling the timber, work which also put damaging strain on the remaining tracks that hadn't been ripped up.

In 2014 Mac stepped in, brought in helpers like Nikki, and the Teifi Valley Railway was reborn with next to nothing. As the track was unusable the miniature 'Pixie Line' saved the railway by entertaining children whilst the big railway started to rebuild after its years of destruction.

The Teifi Valley Railway, Nikki told me, is quite unique; it's a heritage railway aiming to recreate and regenerate not a working passenger railway for tourist purposes, more a railway aiming to recreate and regenerate a heritage railway. In short, they are starting from scratch with few assets and just a hardy, determined gang of volunteers trying to keep the line alive for the next generation.

I joined the two elderly people from the northeast straddling the carriage on the little train, driven by Mac himself, of course. Mac then showed me around his sheds, where the railway's two steam locomotives sit enjoying a painfully slow restoration. There had been a further tragedy, you see. The society's Chief Engineer had slipped onto his father's stairlift, breaking vertebrae in his back and, now wheelchair-bound, was unable to physically do the work required to bring the railway's pride and joy, Sergeant Murphy, back into action that year (2019). Many offers for Sergeant Murphy had been received from other railways, arguing that the locomotive could be better used elsewhere, but the Teifi Valley had stuck to their guns, holding onto their final big asset, determined that one day the line would be restored to its former glory, with a steam train of some infamy puffing through the woods.

Sergeant Murphy was built in 1918 and is famed as the locomotive that killed its driver when it overturned in a quarry in 1932. Whilst we'll have to wait a little while longer for Murphy to reappear from its shed, a trip on the big railway, again driven by Mac and with Margaret now having discarded her pinny for her conductor's cap, was like a journey back to the beginning of railway preservation. Reaching the end of the useable track, Mac and I walked along the overgrown trackbed where

the tracks had been lifted. He showed me the tantalising hundred or so yards requiring sleepers and track that would allow him to rebuild his railway across the worst part to Pontprenshitw. The line beyond is in decent nick. If they can bridge the small gap they and get their steam locos working again, the Teifi Valley is back in business.

At the Teifi Valley Railway they haven't got much. Apart from love and hope and belief.

Chapter 31 - North Wales in a Nutshell

I t's before 7am. There is an autumnal chill in the air, but it's forecast to become a sunny September day. I'm stood at Llandudno's Coach Park, a road behind the resort's sweeping promenade and bay, lined with hotels as far as the eye can see, waiting for the number 5 Arriva bus. It's called the Cymru Coastliner and it will take me to Caernarfon.

This was another Welsh recce, covering the last few parts of the itinerary ahead of personally leading my German group around Wales a few weeks later. The group would have the comfort of a coach transfer to meet the Welsh Highland Railway beneath the keeps of Caernarfon Castle, but today I would have to make my own way there for the start of a classic round trip through Snowdonia. By the way, it also serves as a fantastic tip for anyone staying in Llandudno who fancies leaving their car behind for the day to explore the mountains, as long as you don't mind skipping breakfast at your hotel.

As far as bus journeys go, and let's face it that's not what this book is about, it has its moments. It cuts through neighbouring Conwy with its castle, then offers more than a glimpse of the North Welsh coast and Anglesey across the Menai Strait as it flits between villages to Bangor, then Caernarfon.

Caernarfon is a town worthy of more than the hour I had to explore. The castle is an impenetrable Welsh icon and nearby is Castle Square with its statues of former Prime Minister David Lloyd George and Sir Hugh Owen, the 19th century education reformist who strove to bring better education to the masses in Wales. In need of some sustenance ahead of the next stage, I headed for some breakfast.

You know the pub chain. There's one in every town. They offer basic food and drink, and are good value for money for those who are kind to company expenses. But, for Barnier and Boris's sake could I just possibly once have a Brexit-free breakfast? I'm not being political. That's not what this is about. Whatever your views on Brexit, I think most of us by that stage were sick of it interfering with our every waking moment. But there is a pub chain that serves Brexit with your beer, Brexit with your bacon butty and No Deal with your Two for One meal. It's enough to make you want to…erm…leave!

At this point, whilst I'm on my soapbox, I'd like to dispel the myth that Welsh people switch from English to Welsh when you walk in the room so that they can talk about you. How many times have I heard this? In Gwynedd around two thirds of the population speak Welsh as well as English. On the bus to Caernarfon and in the pub I heard people of all ages speaking their own language, just going about their daily routine. In one corner of the Dog & Brexit pub there was a bunch of old lads having their regular morning coffee and a chat (probably about chuffing Brexit) in Welsh. In the other corner there was a conversation ongoing in English. The bar staff interchanged between English and Welsh with the ease that only comes with having two mother tongues. So here's my message to English tourists. They aren't talking about you. You're not that interesting. And if they are talking about you in Welsh it's probably because you're being a bit of a dick.

The sun was shining and Caernarfon Castle is a stunning backdrop to the Welsh Highland Railway's modern station, complete with a cool café and shop. I wandered along the platform to watch the loco taking on water before readying itself for the ride. A coach group had reserved a carriage a few back from the steam loco, but I headed for the one behind the cab, the steam enthusiasts' favoured place on any steam train, where, with windows down, you can hear the pounding of the engine as it tackles the terrain and smell the smoke and soot from its toil. After Waunfawr station the views to the left open up spectacularly. The Snowdonian scenery is splendid and you can really understand why this railway has been described as one of the best in the world.

Llyn Cwellyn appears on the right hand side to satisfy those at the other window (though I had the whole carriage and all the windows to myself!). Then comes the Aberglaslyn Valley, on the right hand side too, with watery woodlands once voted Britain best view! Tunnels engineered through the mountains finally return us to the coast at Porthmadog.

Porthmadog itself is a pleasant town, but its station, home to the Welsh Highland Railway and the Ffestiniog Railway, is so well equipped that it is pointless venturing far. The onsite pub provided a between trains local beer on the patio next to the platforms in the Indian Summer September sunshine for this traveller who had left his car at home, as both railways geared up for their next trip up into the mountains.

My next part of this round trip would be on the Ffestiniog. Okay, if it's not quite as scenic as the Welsh Highland Railway, it's certainly just as interesting. Coming out of Porthmadog there are fantastic seascapes on the right, then views open up again on the right hand side after Tan-Y-Bwch. But that's not all as there follows something unique in British heritage railway circles, the word 'circle' being apt. At Dduallt Loop the track spirals the mountain to conquer the inhospitable terrain. As the train climbs towards the eerie gleaming grey mountains of Blaenau Ffestiniog, waterfalls cascade outside your window to the left.

The history of these two narrow gauge railways is filled with controversy and politics that I won't attempt to cover here. Let's just say that the Welsh Highland Railway, extended to Caernarfon to make use of its full potential in 2011, is at 25 miles in length an extraordinary experience that you shouldn't miss. Rheilffordd Eyri in Welsh, Eyri referring to Snowdonia, the land of eagles, its history as a struggling slate and passenger carrying railway has been transformed into a tourist gem. The Ffestiniog Railway, shorter at just over 13 miles long and very much built to transport the slate hewn from the mountains, is the oldest surviving railway company in the world. The whole trip, if you can manage it, is well worth a day of anyone's time.

The round trip doesn't end there though. At Blaenau Ffestiniog you simply walk across the tracks to the main station, from where Transport for Wales operates regular…ish services through the Conwy Valley to the seaside town of Llandudno. The Conwy Valley Line runs for 27 miles and was also originally built to transport slate, this time to the seaport at Deganwy. At the time part of the London & North Western Railway, it has been a challenge to keep the railway open in recent times, with parts of the line washed out by the Welsh weather. Leaving Blaenau Ffestiniog you get better views of the slate mountains than on the Ffestiniog Railway, on that particular day glistening in the late summer sun. A two mile tunnel bores through the mountain as the line descends towards Betws Y Coed, with lovely valley views all the way on both sides of the train. As the journey progresses you need to try to position yourself to the left though, as watery landscapes turn to seascapes after Deganwy.

Back in Llandudno at just after 4.15pm, the day's circular tour complete, the weather was still warm and sunny. Warm and sunny enough for one last great railway adventure. From Llandudno's striking promenade and pier a short walk takes you to Victoria Station, the base of the Great Orme Tramway, opened in 1902 and now the only remaining cable-operated street tramway in Britain. With a quick change at the middle station, the tramway operates with original vehicles dating from its very beginnings, taking you through the streets, up severe inclines to the top of the Great Orme. This is the only place in the country that springs to my mind where you can be sitting on the beach enjoying an ice cream one minute, then feeling the breeze with a soothing hot chocolate at the top of a mountain just a few minutes later. A truly wonderful way to top off a wonderful day. Croeso I Gymru. Welcome to Wales.

Chapter 32 - EuroCities – Berlin to Prague

'So, Englishman! You think you've got palaces? We're going to show you some real palaces!'

This would have been early 1992, about half-way through my year out in Germany, an obligatory part of my German degree course. I had been living with a chaotic but kind family in a rural village near Bremerhaven where nothing much happened. The family father, Johann, had been promising all week that we would go on an excursion, would not tell me where but insisted that we would be leaving at 5am. Where the hell were they taking me?!

Berlin and I go back a long way, you see. And, boy, was it a long way. The palaces Johann was boasting about were five hours' drive away in Potsdam. And what a drive. Two years after the fall of the Berlin Wall, this did not look like a unified country. We drove along rickety roads in eerie East German villages, happening often upon the Russian army, who were still to vacate their former Soviet sister state, whose soldiers wore exotic big caps and whose vehicles pumped out thick black smoke.

We made it to Sanssouci and Neues Palais, the ostentatious 'Prussian Versailles' in Potsdam, before spending a couple of hours in East Berlin, where I bought a piece of the Wall (or a piece of someone's wall, at any rate!) and gawped at the bullet holes in the building facades, a reminder of the street battles for Berlin nearly 50 years earlier and which had never been renovated by the GDR.

I have been back maybe fifteen times since, mostly with work, and so have usually done my sightseeing at night. On my last trip, just before the 2020 pandemic happened, I managed some daytime sightseeing. I am particularly intrigued with the former East Berlin, what was beyond the Wall, and I thought I would share with you my tour of the Unter den Linden grand avenue, along with a couple of tips off the beaten track.

We begin just beyond our virtual Berlin Wall at the Reichstag building. It was built late 19th century to house the German parliament. After the abdication of Kaiser Wilhelm II the new republic was proclaimed in 1918 by Social Democrat Philipp Scheidemann from a Reichstag balcony. In 1933 you probably know that the Reichstag caught fire, which gave the Nazis an excuse to seize power. Following World War II the building lay unused by the East German government. Restored and redesigned by British architect Norman Foster, the Reichstag is once again the united Germany's parliament.

A short walk brings us to the Brandenburg Gate, built at the behest of the powerful Prussian monarch Frederick the Great in the 18th century, the gateway to Berlin's grand avenue. Beside it is the Holocaust Memorial, a must-visit installation. From the roadside it looks like a series of shallow slabs. What you can only experience by walking into the memorial is that the ground sinks, the slabs eventually towering above you, suffocating daylight, swallowing you up. I challenge you to not walk away from here deeply moved. It is a powerful attack on your senses.

After walking past the embassies and the swish Adlon Hotel, a short detour takes us to the 'Palace of Tears' at Friedrichstrasse station. In an era when families, friends and love affairs were separated by the Wall, this was the point where any visit from loved ones in the West ended. The last hug, the last kiss, before divided lives continued amidst the madness of a city partitioned.

Further up Unter den Linden is the German State Opera. The square beside this house of culture was the site of an act of cultural crime. It was here in 1933 that Nazi students burned books that didn't adhere to the new ideology. On a tablet in the square is a quotation from the German 19th century poet, Heinrich Heine. 'In the place where they burn books, they will eventually burn people'. I know of no city as thought-provoking as Berlin.

Onwards to Berlin Cathedral and, next door, a sight that most tours won't visit. The Radisson Hotel has a fishtank in its lobby. 'That's not unusual,' I hear you say. Well, how about a floor to ceiling aquarium? Where else in Berlin can you book a room with sea view?!

On previous visits 'Palace Square' had been a waste ground. Originally the site of the Prussian monarchy's Berlin Palace, in GDR times the site was rebuilt as the concrete monstrosity East German parliament, Palast der Republik, a place so hated that it was pulled down after reunification. Palace Square lay empty for many years. In its place, finally, they are just completing the rebuild of the original Berlin Palace. Berlin is coming full circle.

A stroll past the 'Red Town Hall' and through the quaint Nikolaiviertel quarter brings us to Alexanderplatz, the former central square of East Berlin with its World Clock and TV Tower. It is here that East Berliners pre the fall of the Wall were reminded of the time in places all over the world that they weren't allowed to visit!

If we jump on an S-Bahn train now at Alexanderplatz, I can take you to Warschauer Strasse, where you can see the lovely Oberbaum Bridge, separating Kreuzberg in what was West Berlin and Friedrichshain in what was East Berlin. After the fall of the Wall I once heard a story that the residents of Kreuzberg and Friedrichshain would enjoy a massive tug of war across the bridge, but I don't know if that's true or just a ropey made-up old tale. Certainly not made up is the East Side Gallery, just a short walk away and one of the last few remaining stretches of the Berlin Wall.

Further east and well off the beaten track is Treptower Park, again accessed via Berlin's superb S-Bahn trains. It is essentially the resting place of the Soviet soldiers who died in the ferocious battles for Berlin and now a memorial park, with a series of concrete slabs depicting the battles for Berlin from the Soviet perspective. On the side of each slab is a quotation from a certain J. Stalin.

The bombastic centrepiece of Treptower Park is a Soviet soldier cradling a German babe in one arm, a sword in the other, boots crushing a swastika! Berlin is a great city for sightseeing, shopping and is great value too. Yet around every corner, in every nook and cranny, there is amazing and thought-provoking history. Berlin is a unique place. I know I will be back again, but for now I need to get to Dresden.

I would always recommend EC or EuroCity services for this route, particularly EC 172 and 173, otherwise known as 'The Hungaria', which still plies the long-distance route from Hamburg to Budapest daily, also calling at Berlin, Dresden and Prague.

There is still something magical for me about travelling through central Europe, just something I can't quite put my finger on. Maybe it's a childhood nostalgia for places that were out of our grasp behind the Iron Curtain, countries we saw glimpses of on European football nights back in the 70s and 80s. Honved, Red Star Belgrade, Steaua Bucharest; vast empty concrete bowls rather than stadia with lines of grey-looking soldiers in uniforms and big caps sitting on the freezing terraces where the spectators should have been. Maybe I am psychologically looking back on a childhood staring at Aunty Monica and Uncle Phillip's atlas at countries sometimes mentioned on John Craven's Newsround, but so far from my own reality then that they may as well have been from another planet.

EC stands for EuroCity. It is the international version of InterCity, born out of cross-border co-operation between rail operators. Its predecessor was the Trans Europ Express (or TEE for short) network, which now conjures up a romance of international rail travel luxury of a bygone age, the 1950s to the 1990s to be exact. Well, it does in my brain at any rate! Speed, luxury, border crossings, mysterious destinations, maybe with a long-distance flirtation, or perhaps just a hint of high intrigue en route. It's almost a film plot. Actually, 'Trans Europe Express' was also a film plot, a mid-1960s movie by Alain Robbe- Grillet.

The EuroCity network, whilst lacking the je ne sais quoi of its predecessor to warrant a French movie script, does still conjure up a certain nostalgia for me. In Germany the InterCity and EuroCity trains live in the shadow of Deutsche Bahn's gleaming superstar ICEs. Inter City Expresses connect the major cities at speeds unimaginable to us in the UK and with all mod cons to boot. By contrast, for me a ride on a slowcoach (by comparison) EuroCity route to central Europe created not long after the fall of the Iron Curtain on train stock from MAV, the Hungarian national train operator, is one filled with memories and nostalgia from a time when those countries were beginning to open up to tourists from the West. What's more, to be part of the EuroCity network the services have to adhere to a certain standard of speed, comfort and catering, preferably with dining car. What's not to like?

I first came to Dresden in the late 1990s on a work trip with a coach tour operator. We were driving around that company's brand new 'Berlin, Dresden & Leipzig' tour, the Operations Manager driving, the guy who would be driving the coach all season in the passenger seat, taking in as much as he could, and me in the back, pointing out the things he should know for his commentary.

Dresden's Old Town is new, of course. The damage caused by the bombing raids was extensive and the city was painstakingly rebuilt after the war. Its main attractions were there in force even back then before the Millennium, apart from one, the Frauenkirche (Church of our Lady), which was still under reconstruction, though it is now back to its former glory. The Zwinger Palace, the Semper Opera House, the Catholic Church all lined up along the river for a dreamy cityscape made famous in Canaletto paintings. This city is known as 'the Florence of the Elbe'.

Dresden, like much of Saxony and the east of Germany, was a hotbed for local hero Martin Luther's reformation and so the presence of such a prominent Catholic church warrants a bit of investigation. The most famous Saxon noble was called 'Augustus the Strong', a chap with regal ideas above his station, becoming King of Poland and requiring conversion to Catholicism. During the same era the Protestant majority in Saxony built the Frauenkirche, towering over the king's church. It was a bit of a message to the monarch from his people, I guess. Since rebuilt and reconsecrated, the golden orb sitting atop the Frauenkirche's gigantic dome was significantly made by a London goldsmith whose father had been in the aircrew that took part in the Dresden bombing raids, part of the healing of the past and bringing the story full circle.

It is worth staying a while, not least to ride the heritage steam lines that rattle through the Saxon countryside, such as the very charming

Weisseritztalbahn from Freital to Dippoldiswalde. Said to be Germany's oldest operational narrow-gauge railway still open to the public, the steam locos haul museum-piece carriages along the scenic Red Weisseritz river valley, which was flowing fast when I was there, up into the Ore Mountains. Badly damaged in the 2002 floods that wreaked havoc on the region, including Dresden and many other central European cities, the line reopened bit by bit, now reaching as far as the mountain spa of Kipsdorf, not far from the Czech border.

'Did you enjoy your Maritim breakfast?' asked the sales manager.

I had stayed overnight at Dresden's Maritim Hotel, enjoying its lavish breakfast buffet, before plonking myself in the lobby waiting for the rather cocky sales manager to arrive. It had always been a toss-up between two very similar standard hotels within a stone's throw of eachother, the Maritim or the Westin Bellevue across the river.

'Yes, I did thanks.'

'Have you ever had breakfast at the Westin Bellevue?' he then enquired.

'Well, no, I haven't.'

'Give me two minutes. Meet me out front at my car. We'll go and compare the Westin breakfast.'

Bold as brass, we walked through to the breakfast room of the Westin Bellevue. Maritim's sales manager knew all the staff at the Westin, greeting them all as we passed, with no attempts to hide the name badge of the rival hotel on his lapel. It was a good buffet, but clearly not as lavish as the Maritim breakfast my driver was so proud of. Point scoring masterclass concluded, little did he know my next meeting was at the Westin and he had inadvertently given me a free lift there. Thanks mate!

The train journey from Dresden to Prague is the most scenic part of 'The Hungaria' EuroCity route. Running right through the heart of Saxon Switzerland, the tracks reach the River Elbe around Pirna, a pleasant and prosperous riverside town, but one of those places that holds a dark secret. The sanatorium here was one of six sites used by the Nazis to trial killing by gas. Their victims at Sonnenstein Palace were some of the most vulnerable people in their own midst, the mentally ill. Labelled unworthy of life by their murderers, 13,000 perished. What's more, Sonnenstein became a school of unfeeling terror, of conditioning people to accept as the norm the very worst acts imaginable, often against the most vulnerable. This was a training ground for mass murder; Franz Stangl, camp commandant of Treblinka Extermination Camp, in whose hands rest the murder of almost a million poor souls, began his journey at one of the six original camps.

Further upstream the sheer cliffs of Bastei are visible from the track. These are the Elbe Sandstone Mountains of Saxon Switzerland. If you have time to explore away from the tracks, there is a beautiful sandstone bridge linking some of the jagged rocks, one of which towers 305 metres above sea level.

240 metres above the Elbe a little further upstream is Königstein Fortress, a stunning hillside fort set atop a table-mountain for high, impregnable drama. This place was never conquered and from the battlements I was amazed by the views of Saxon Switzerland, the Elbe far below and the Czech Republic in the distance beyond Bad Schandau, another point at which you could alight to sample the Kirnitzschtal Tramway, the only one serving a German National Park.

Entering the Czech Republic the train continues to hug the Elbe along a green, scenic river valley to Děčín, then Ústí Nad Labem and Litomerice. The pretty Bohemian scenery eventually gives way to Prague. There are few cities more alluring, but what is the secret of that allure? Most great cities have a river running through them (tick). Maybe a famous bridge spanning said river (tick). A proud castle perhaps, standing protectively above the town (tick). How about a beautiful open square flanked by a series of stunning buildings in several architectural styles? Yes, you guessed it, Prague ticks that box too.

You can tick off all the above on foot, plus the house of Franz Kafka, sing Good King Wenceslas in the chapel of the good king himself at St Vitas Cathedral, walk over the Charles Bridge, then marvel at Old Town Square with its astronomical clock, the Gothic Tyn Church and, by stark contrast, the rococo Kinsky Palace. All in one morning, if you like. Phew.

Prague is compact and you can enjoy all those lovely cultural, touristy things, then a hearty stodgy meal of meat, dumplings and cabbage in a quiet backstreet tavern. Even if you need to spend your days rushing from hotel to hotel, you can still sample the dark beer and dumpling deliciousness of Prague's brewery taverns after dark. U Fleků is my favourite, a historic and homely house dating from 1499. The Croatian football team Hajduk Split was formed here in 1908, as described in another chapter, and you can imagine putting the world to rights amidst the echoes and chatter in this traditional tavern.

Speaking of hotels, I once spent a couple of days racing around Prague, trying to replace a hotel that one of the directors had disliked. I visited hotel after hotel, never finding anywhere I liked as much as the one I was charged with replacing. It might not have been in the ideal location, but for me it was a no-brainer. We were making rail holidays and this was a hotel with its own railway! The main building and the executive floor up the hill were connected by a funicular, rather than bog-standard lift or stairs. Imagine riding the rails to and from your hotel room. It just so happens that I stayed there too and, well, you might have guessed already that I tried it out a few times during my stay.

Chapter 33 - Only Settle for the Best

For me lots of things began in Leeds. Independence, for a start, as I began a course many moons ago as a teenager studying German at Leeds University. I suppose my first cookery disasters happened in Leeds whilst trying hopelessly to fend for myself. My first romantic disasters happened there too. I think I improved on both those scores. You will have to ask my wife, I guess, a Leeds lass I met a few years after I had left the city. We met in travel, Maeve and I. We met at Leger Holidays, a coach holiday company in my Rotherham hometown and our careers have criss-crossed, more than once at rail holiday companies. I'm glad that she read the signals, asking me out on a date. All these years later we still haven't hit the buffers, plus we have too miniature versions to show for our time spent in the sidings.

Our first rail holiday as a couple also began in Leeds. In the early days of our courtship we bought a weekend hop-on hop-off ticket between Leeds and Carlisle, with a couple of nights booked above a pub in Settle that quickly became a favourite. It was a chance to explore the Settle & Carlisle Line, endangered for years despite its obvious touristic draw, a railway through the spine of the north country, skirting the Yorkshire Dales, crossing bleak moors of Brontë-esque beauty and descending through Westmorland into Cumbria and border country.

But there is so much to see even before you reach Settle, tracks we've covered so many times since. After Shipley the train stops at Saltaire, the company town built by Sir Titus Salt and a living, breathing complete Victorian village. It is not surprisingly a UNESCO World Heritage site, with Salt's Mill now accommodating exhibitions by famous local lad done good, David Hockney, and housing, civic buildings and parks not altered since their heyday.

Beyond the sturdy stonework of Salt's model village for model workers, a local feud has been raging over the years. With a few of my groups visiting Saltaire I had contacted two possible guides, the village's History Club and a commercial company offering historical guiding in period dress. We chose the latter as they seemed, well, more fun! A missive was received from the History Club chairman, telling us our customers would be 'entertained but misinformed' and that we were a 'commercial company that didn't care'. A quick look on their website showed an embittered and very personal feud for the 'truth'.

Truth is usually about opinion and interpretation. In truth, the customers loved the allegedly entertaining, misinforming, non-factual guided tour of Saltaire in period dress by an engaging and charming woman. We'll never know what the History Club's 'Mythbuster' tour was like.

If you walk across the Leeds Liverpool Canal and the River Aire, then through Roberts Park you reach a little-known gem, the Shipley Glen Tramway, dating from 1895 and claiming to be Britain's oldest working cable tramway. Check before visiting that it will be open, but if you catch them on an operating day it's an extra little treat, pulling you up a quarter of a mile to Shipley Glen, self-styled as Britain's first theme park. The Victorian-era pleasure grounds are long gone but the glen itself marks the start point of lovely walks.

Back on the service train, four minutes later we jump out at Bingley, an unassuming West Yorkshire mill town, where a short walk takes us to another engineering masterpiece, Five Rise Locks, a lock staircase and probably the biggest highlight on the Leeds Liverpool Canal. The locks have been described as one of the 'Seven Wonders of the Waterways'. There are actually two lock staircases here, both dating from 1774, with Three Rise Locks encountered first, before a walk along the towpath brings us to the main attraction, a unique five-rise staircase with a total elevation of 60 feet.

You can rejoin the train at Cottingley or walk back down to Bingley after having a breather in the lockside café. But before you can say in your best Yorkshire accent, 'Eeh by gum, lad, what's the next treat?' just a few minutes later we are in Keighley, where you could spend a whole day on the Keighley & Worth Valley Railway, pootling along the edge of the Yorkshire Dales into Brontë Country. In fact, I'd highly recommend that you do exactly that, a whole day exploring the five-mile former branch line with a day rover ticket, hopping on and off as you please. At Ingrow there's the little museum of the line, included in your day rover ticket. You can spot the backdrops of the classic movie 'The Railway Children', which was filmed at the Keighley & Worth Valley Railway, not least at the perfectly pretty Oakworth Station, often voted the best preserved railway station in the country. The real jewel in the crown is Haworth though, home of the Brontë family, where you must visit the Brontë Parsonage Museum. Oh and who can forget the sight of the Tour de France peloton heaving its way up Haworth's iconic cobbled Main Street past the Post Office and the Black Bull before tackling the nearby Cote d'Oxenhope Moor. By 'eck and zut alors!

Back in Keighley, I admit it has been thirsty work. As we conveniently left the car at home, maybe there is time to try a sneaky pint of Timothy Taylor's ales. Taylor's is, after all, the traditional independent Yorkshire brewery that has spawned not one but five Champion Beer of Britain awards (Madonna's favourite beer, Landlord, in 1982, 1983, 1994 and 1999, and Boltmaker in 2014).

Around fifteen minutes later we reach Skipton. I thought long and hard about whether or not to skip Skipton. When all's said and done, we are supposed to be exploring the iconic Settle & Carlisle line, but at this rate we'll never reach Settle! Try as I might, I just can't skip Skipton, the lovely market town at the gateway to the Yorkshire Dales. The castle, the famous pork pies, the boats trips on the Leeds & Liverpool Canal, the Embsay & Bolton Abbey Steam Railway departing from the nearby village of Embsay to another beauty spot. Writing this reminiscence from Covid-19 lockdown, I was actually waiting patiently for my next trip there to see the latest jewel in Skipton's crown. You see, I recently got a phone call from Malcolm.

Malcolm is the owner of the Rendez-Vous Hotel, a friendly abode on the canal towpath just outside of town. He is a much-loved local personality, no slouch at 86 years of age, in fact you could say larger than life figure. He is also in possession of 'Graceful Swan', a brand-new electric-powered dining boat offering a unique culinary experience along the canal, seating up to 60 people. The panoramic windows, the lack of noisy motor, as Malcolm spoke my mind floated effortlessly along with him. But we'll park that one for later, or maybe we should moor it instead. After all, we still haven't reached Settle!

Chapter 34 - All aboard the Staycation Express!

'**A**nyone wishing to leave the train at Dent, please be aware that Dent village is nearly five miles from the station. There is, however, a bus connection to Kendal. Once a week.'

Our humorous and unassuming train host, Anthony, was in full flow as the 'Staycation Express' approached Dent, at 1150 feet above sea level the highest mainline station in England and not actually a scheduled stop on this service. From our start point at Appleby's delightfully pretty station in the rolling Westmorland countryside the train had fought hostile yet heavenly terrain, heaving slowly up to the line's highest point at Aisgill. At Garsdale, if you are quick, you can spot the statue of border collie Ruswarp (pronounced 'Russup'), the only dog to object to the closure of the scenic Settle & Carlisle Line when the railway's own end of the line loomed in the 1980s. Up in the moors, in blissful isolation, with roads sparse and wildlife abundant, I felt thankful to faithful old Ruswarp and the 32,000 human objectors who kept this line alive.

This little excursion was a big step for me. After a lifetime travelling, making rail holidays for a living, a few months 'off the rails' and shielding at home from Covid-19 had resulted in itchy feet. Back out in the wide world, the 'Staycation Express' seemed too good an opportunity to miss, revisiting the line that Mrs C and I had discovered during our early days of courtship. The brainchild of Rail Charter Services, when lockdown was lifted in summer 2020 this special timetabled tourist service pulled former first class Inter City carriages three times a day in each direction across the stunning Settle & Carlisle Line. You could join the train in Skipton or Settle at the southern end, whereas Appleby was the excursion's northern terminus. Whilst not luxurious, the seating was spacious and comfortable, each seat coming with a table and positioned by a picture window to view the Pennines in all their changeable glory. Seating was arranged with four seats with table on one side of the aisle and two seats with table on the other side, each bay separated by unobtrusive perspex screens to conform with the unusual times we were living through. At stations, boarding and when walking around the train I wore my facemask, a train design (of course!) hand-made by my youngest daughter, the very crafty Clare. Otherwise, you could sit back mask-free and enjoy a little bit of nostalgia and escapism amidst the moorland heather.

After Dent came more drama. Our train trundled slowly above the 24 arches of the Ribblehead Viaduct, over 100 feet above the valley, the line crossing between Whernside, Ingleborough and Pen-y-ghent, Yorkshire's 'Three Peaks'. Brooding clouds added to the drama before our descent through Ribblesdale to glorious sunshine at Settle, a gorgeous town in the Yorkshire Dales from where Malham, Grassington and the Ingleton Falls are just a short ride away.

Back in the market town of Skipton, itself a great base for exploring Yorkshire, the news broke that the UK's Covid-19 quarantine regulations would be widened to include France and the Netherlands amongst other countries. It felt pretty apt to have spent that same day enjoying the bleak beauty of this island on a train called the 'Staycation Express'!

Chapter 35 - Transpennine Excess

This final chapter is about home. Okay, not specifically my childhood home, which was Rotherham, but about the north of England. Wherever I've travelled, I am always somehow drawn back. I've lived in Germany and France, but I always came back, to Sheffield, Leeds and even Accrington, which from where I'm sitting is the wrong side of the Pennines.

As a Yorkshire lad I was always the butt of the jokes amongst my many good pals in that Lancashire mill town, all good-humoured of course.

'What's the best thing to come out of Yorkshire?'

'The M62 into Lancashire!'

If I had a pound for every time I heard this little joke during the three years I lived in Lancashire I would be a rich man. All the more so, of course, due to the fact that, as a Yorkshireman, we all have short arms, deep pockets. Well, according to everyone I ever met in Lancashire anyway.

I ended my time in Lancashire teaching German in Further Education Colleges and often opened my first lesson with adult classes with the ice-breaker, 'I'm Rob and I'm a Yorkshireman!' Usually there would be a few gentle jibes, a bit of welcome friendly banter, but I made the mistake of trying the same ice-breaker with a BTEC class of 16 year olds. 'Baaaaaaaa!!' they all went. All 30 of them. A cacophony of sheep noises. Despite the fact that I'm from industrial South

Yorkshire and outside the Burnley College classroom window behind the students I could see sheep on them thuuurrr Lancashire hills. Bloody kids.

'What car do you drive, sir?' asked one surly Burnley youth to my right after the sheep noises had ceased.

'Why do you ask?' replied your friendly Yorkshire teacher.

'So I can put a bomb under it next week!' came the menacing response. Well, as menacing as a gawky 16 year old with bumfluff round his chops could muster.

The class guffawed.

'You'll struggle with that, pal. I don't drive!'

Game, set and match to the teacher.

It was in Lancashire that I picked up my habit of being the first to the bar, trying desperately to dispel the stereotype of the tight Yorkshireman. I feel as deeply affectionate to towns and cities across the Pennines as I do for those in 'God's County' or whatever annoying terminology we Tykes decide to use to assume our perceived superiority. It's about people, ultimately, and we aren't very different, despite the marked change of regional accent from town to town.

The first time I set foot on a train was in the 1970s at primary school. I remember very little about it now, except that it was definitely one of the best things to come out of Yorkshire, the line from Sheffield to Manchester via Chinley, the Hope Valley Line. I presume we were taken to Sheffield to join the train, trundling through the 3 ½ mile long Totley Tunnel on our way to Grindleford, where we sketched the western entrance of the tunnel from the platform.

If this sounds a bit, well, sketchy, but it was a long time ago. We'll come back to tunnels a little later, but, writing this final chapter from lockdown due to the Covid-19 pandemic, I am missing travel and also the gentle pleasures of a traditional pub. For this last chapter about home, I thought I would treat you to a journey across the Pennines, with a couple of choice diversions, and some special resting places, should you have an hour between trains.

Starting in Liverpool, if you had a little time on your hands, a walk down to the docks might bring you to the Baltic Fleet, a brewpub in a Grade II listed traditional building, clinging dearly to its heritage and shining with beauty amidst high-rise Johnny-come-lately developments. Or, of course, there is the famous Phil, or the Philharmonic Dining Rooms, a Victorian gem named after the concert hall across the road, which lays claim to being Britain's most ornate pub. But if you haven't got much time between trains, the Grade II listed Crown Hotel just outside Lime Street Station ticks the boxes too for ornate interior, traditional exterior (with its Walkers Ales of Warrington sign) and a selection of good ales.

There are several options to connect Liverpool to Manchester, none of which are particularly fast, so I'm stepping onto the stopping train at Lime Street. The Liverpool & Manchester Railway opened in 1830, the world's first inter-city service and the first to solely use steam locomotives. The opening of the railway was famously overshadowed by the death of Liverpool MP William Huskisson, who was run over by The Rocket in a bizarre accident.

There isn't the greatest selection of watering holes around Piccadilly these days since it was regenerated. My tip would be to spend a bit longer in Manchester, hop out at Deansgate or Oxford Road and take in the traditional delights of the Peveril of the Peak or Briton's Protection instead. I first went to the latter back in the 1990s when my friend's band played upstairs. As memorable as they were, my abiding memory is of local media star and founder of Factory Records, Anthony H Wilson, swanning around the room. He watched the absolutely godawful arty-farty support act, then left before my mate's brilliant band entered the stage, who were about to sign to a very famous independent label. Whilst Tony Wilson was responsible for bringing the world Joy Division, New Order and the Happy Mondays, maybe this explains some of the terrible signings he made for Factory, whilst missing out on The Smiths!

The Briton's Protection takes its name from a past as an army recruitment venue and is a Grade II listed building. What makes the pub most interesting, aside from its little snug rooms, choice of real ales and 200 whiskies, are the murals on the walls depicting the Peterloo Massacre, which took place on the adjacent St Peter's Fields in 1819, a momentous and tragic day for Manchester that is barely commemorated anywhere else in the city. Whilst the Briton's

Protection isn't per se a station pub, it is close to the Manchester Central Exhibition Centre, which uses the original building of the former station of the same name. The old station hotel, the fabulous Midland, still exists and is well worth a visit. And if you have a little more time you can even take a wander to the former Liverpool Road Station, former terminus since 1830 of the Liverpool & Manchester Railway, the oldest surviving station building in the world, which now forms part of the Manchester Science Museum.

From Manchester Piccadilly let's jump back on the Transpennine Express to the next stop, leaving the metropolitan sprawl for the Tameside satellite town of Stalybridge, where you don't need to leave the station. The station's original refreshment rooms, now called the Stalybridge Buffet Bar, date from 1885 and are one of the few remaining Victorian station buffets left unscathed by time. Here you can settle by a roaring fire between trains, slurp a pint of their good selection of real ales and enjoy a hearty bite to eat, surrounded by railwayana and Victoriana befitting a museum, not to mention the original ceiling of the 1st Class Ladies' Waiting Room.

Deliberately taking the slow stopping train from Stalybridge across the Pennines towards Huddersfield gives plenty of time to see the hills and vales of the England's backbone of hills. At the Lancashire village of Diggle, where the station is long gone, the train enters Standedge Tunnel, re-emerging near Marsden in Yorkshire. Before the train slouches towards Huddersfield we alight at Marsden itself for an extra treat.

Marsden is an unassuming Pennine town that spawned the current Poet Laureate, Simon Armitage. In fact, these green and grey hills of West Yorkshire have a knack for producing poets, with Ted Hughes originating from the Calderdale village of Mytholmroyd, just across the M62. Whilst there's a station pub here, we'll by-pass it. The relatively short walk along the towpath of the Huddersfield Narrow Canal brings us back to Standedge itself. If you don't fancy the walk and are lucky, there is a very occasional water taxi from Marsden Station to Standedge, operated by Huddersfield Canal Society volunteers.

After a pleasant walk we reach Standedge Tunnel and its visitor centre, run by the Canal & River Trust, commemorating the history and construction of Britain's longest, deepest and highest canal tunnel. What you are met with isn't one tunnel though, as there are four parallel tunnels hewn into the Pennine rock between here and Diggle. The canal tunnel came first, opening in 1811, followed by a single track rail tunnel in 1848 and another single track rail tunnel in 1871. These tunnels weren't sufficient to ease the bottleneck of cross-Pennine rail traffic back then, and so a double track rail tunnel was built too, opening in 1894. Only the canal tunnel and the 1894 rail tunnel are in use today, although the two closed rail tunnels have been maintained, to the point where it has been suggested they reopen. If you have time you can take a narrowboat trip into the tunnel. Otherwise, after a quick look at the Visitor Centre's excellent display, the canalside café serves excellent food and a welcome cuppa.

From Marsden our train descends to Huddersfield via the excellently Yorkshirely named Slawit, or Slaithwaite to non-locals. Huddersfield is a rare treat for the thirsty traveller not wishing to venture far from the station with two pubs accessible from platform 1. The once distinguished woollen town's rather grand classical station façade is bookended by what were the symmetrically built ticket halls of two rival railways, now both converted into pubs. It is worth venturing out onto St George Square first though to admire the building, the statue of Huddersfield lad made good, Harold Wilson and to take a peek at the George Hotel, now controversially closed for what seems like an eternal refurb, but the historic birthplace of Rugby League in 1895. Looking back at the station frontage, the Head of Steam is in the left hand former ticket hall behind the classical columns. The Kings Head is in the right hand ticket hall and gets my vote for its ornate tiled floor and friendly chatter.

Next stop is Dewsbury, where there isn't quite such a tricky choice but where you can also access a great pub directly from the platform. The West Riding is probably the best pub in town for real ale, hearty bar food, railwayana and a cosy atmosphere. I suppose it's about time we went to Leeds.

I first moved to Leeds as a student in 1989 when it seemed like a dark post-industrial city, unwelcoming to bookish long-haired drips. I enjoyed my student years in Leeds, but slipped home to South

Yorkshire regularly for the comfort blanket of belonging. Leeds didn't feel like home. I left four years later, but moved back in 2001 to live with my very wonderful and understanding wife, a Leodensian. Leeds has been transformed into a cosmopolitan city, with architecture unscathed by war or time like no other major northern industrial centre. Still, for many years Leeds didn't feel like home. Eventually neither did my original home. We had our two amazing daughters, my work travel intensified. I accepted my lot as a displaced person and felt no need to be at home in a place, just with people. This is, I suppose, a traveller's life.

Strangely Leeds does now feel like my home. It took long enough, but it chipped away and eventually won a place in my heart alongside my family. And Leeds Station is the gateway for me, the sigh of relief after any arduous journey, from its leaky days back in my youth to the smart station of today. But don't just stay at Leeds Station. Explore a little. The Corn Exchange, the wonderful Victorian Kirkgate Market, the arcades and the ornate buildings that were spared Nazi bombs. For refreshment, from the pedestrianised Briggate shopping street you will find little alleyways, called 'ginnels' in Leeds, each with its own hostelry. The best is Whitelocks, with its cosy but ornate bar and outdoor seats along the ginnel. The oldest pub in the city, Whitelocks dates back to 1715.

The next stop on our route of transpennine excess would be York, a great railway city and home of the best railway museum in the world. Add to this the Minster, the city walls, the museums, the galleries and the bridges across the Ouse and you have a perfect tourist city. Hell, it's got dozens of great pubs too, plus its own brewery within the city wall, although the York Tap at the station is the perfect place to sit waiting for a delayed train. And, heck, I've had that experience quite a few times! But I'm not going as far as York. My last station is Garforth. Home is where your loved ones live. I'm hopping out here. I hope you've enjoyed the journey and I'm grateful to you for reading. The years in which I write this, 2020 and 2021, are filled with a disconnection, of people moving further apart from one another. Rail travel is a great connector though. Where shall we go next?

Printed in Great Britain
by Amazon

21194483R00130